For Jennie
my good friend + fellow historian, to thank you for your help + encouragement.

Sir William Knighton:
The Strange Career of a Regency Physician

by

Charlotte Frost

Charlotte 8.2.2011

Bright Pen

A Bright Pen Book

Text Copyright © Charlotte Frost
Cover design by © Jamie Day
Front cover: Portrait by Sir Thomas Lawrence, 1823 (Copyright Private Collection)
Back cover: Portrait by Sir David Wilkie, 1835 (Copyright University of Dundee Museum Services, DUNUC ARTS 157)

All rights reserved. No part of this publication may be reproduced, stored in a retrieval system, or transmitted in any form or by any means, electronic, mechanical, photocopy, recording or otherwise, without prior written permission of the copyright owner. Nor can it be circulated in any form of binding or cover other than that in which it is published and without similar condition including this condition being imposed on a subsequent purchaser.

British Library Cataloguing Publication Data.
A catalogue record for this book is available from the British Library

ISBN 978-07552-1301-6

Authors OnLine Ltd
19 The Cinques
Gamlingay, Sandy
Bedfordshire SG19 3NU
England

This book is also available in e-book format, details of which are available at
www.authorsonline.co.uk

Printed and bound in Great Britain by
CPI Antony Rowe, Chippenham and Eastbourne

To Gavin Maidment and Peter Rogers, my first mentors in historical research, for fostering an atmosphere of conviviality and enquiry that has inspired so many of us.

Contents

List of Illustrations	vi
Acknowledgments	vii
Introduction	x
Chapter 1 - 1777–1797: The Farmer's Son	1
Chapter 2 - 1797–1809: The Young Doctor	15
Chapter 3 - 1809–1817: Into Society	28
Chapter 4 - 1817–1822: Into Royal Favour	43
Chapter 5 - Home, Sincerity and Affection	57
Chapter 6 - 1822–1825: The King's Dear Friend	69
Chapter 7 - 1825–1829: A New Friend	81
Chapter 8 - 1829–1830: The Final Year at Court	101
Chapter 9 - Colleague, Friend and Fellow Traveller	110
Chapter 10 - Myth, Mistake and Discrepancy	124
Chapter 11 - 1830–1836: Retirement	137
Illustrations	151
Select Bibliography	155
Index	169

Illustrations

Feather by Mrs Dorothea Knighton, c1801. Plymouth and West Devon Record Office

Sherwood Lodge, anon, 1810. The Georgian Group Pardoe Collection

Blendworth House by Lady Knighton, 1820s. The Georgian Group Pardoe Collection

'The Jew and the doctor; or, secret Influence behind the Curtain!! Vide Times Feby. 19th. 1828', attributed to George Cruikshank, published by John Fairburn, London, February 1828. British Museum

View of Hole's Hole Quay on the Tamar by the Reverend John Swete, 8 April 1793. Devon Record Office

Acknowledgments

I could not have attempted this book without the scholarship of others, especially that of Arthur Aspinall, Robert Potter Berry, Iris Butler, Sir George Clark, Richard Culpin, John M T Ford, Flora Fraser, Austin Gee, Albert Goodwin, Wendy Hinde, Susan C Lawrence, Judith Schneid Lewis, Christopher Lloyd and Jack L S Coulter, Lisa Rosner, Sir Robert Somerville, K S Southam, Harold Temperley, P V Wallis and R V Wallis, and Frances Wilson. Without the intervention of Peter Ardern, Richard Brooks, Val Fontana and Wendy Smith relevant aspects of medical, military and European history would have eluded me. Ailsa Sleigh advised on loans (to George, Prince of Wales, not to me), and authors Tom Ambrose, Gerry Woodcock and Andrew Lambert answered my queries. Henry Engleheart provided information from his family papers. Reverend Nick Law cleared ivy from a tomb to send me a memorial inscription. David Garner provided the illustration of Hole's Hole from Devon Record Office. Timothy Duke of the College of Heralds conducted research on my behalf, as did the Royal Institute of British Architects. Local historians were unfailingly generous. In particular John Merrell gave me access to his local history collection and shared his research on Kensal Green Cemetery, Jennie Stringer advised on midwifery, and Steve Jones shared research from his biographies of Admiral Sir Charles Napier and Admiral Samuel Hood, Viscount Hood.

I am sincerely grateful to all the archives listed in the bibliography for giving me access to their collections, suggesting further research, supplying copy documents and allowing me to reproduce images or quote from documents. In addition Rebecca Saunders at Devon Record Office allowed me access to unconserved documents, without which this book would be much the poorer, and Peter Basham at the Royal College of Physicians, Caroline Lam at King's College, London, Geraldine O'Driscoll at the Royal College of Surgeons, Mark Pomeroy at the Royal Academy, and Nathan Williams at the Museum of English Rural Life all arranged privileged access for me. Access to the Royal Archives was arranged by

Pamela Clark who made me most welcome and gave me valuable advice. In addition Lucy Atkinson of the Museum of English Rural Life, Peter Fleming of the National Army Museum, Katharine Higgon and Katherine Godfrey of King's College, London, and Peter Basham of the Royal College of Physicians answered postal and email queries.

Help also came from archives not listed in the bibliography. Judith Curthoys of Christ Church, Oxford, and Ann Wheeler of Charterhouse Archives provided information about Knighton's son. June Ellner of King's College, Aberdeen, Rachel Hart of the University of St Andrews, and Matti Watson of Lambeth Palace Library researched Knighton's medical qualifications. Local and Naval Studies at Portsmouth Central Library suggested further research and provided access to special collections. City of Portsmouth library service and North End Library, Portsmouth, saved me travel and expense by obtaining books on inter-library loan. Tavistock Museum put me in touch with other researchers. Dr Williams's Library suggested further resources. The Fitzwilliam Museum, and Bedfordshire and Luton Archives and Record Service provided copy documents. Commander Saunders Watson of Rockingham Castle kindly sent me an image of Blendworth House, and I owe special thanks to Roberta Gill, archivist at Rockingham Castle, for answering my queries and for her generous hospitality. Michael Bidnell of The Georgian Group and Marijke Booth of Christie's arranged for me to visit their archives while Jeremy Rex-Parkes of Christie's supplied a copy catalogue. The Witt Library at the Courtauld Institute, the Heinz Archive for Portraiture at the National Portrait Gallery, and the Paul Mellon Centre also allowed me access to their collections. I found much useful material in the Frewen Library at the University of Portsmouth, and it is a privilege and inspiration to use the Institute of Historical Research Library.

Had I been allowed to accept only one piece of advice it would have been that of technical author Ken Pugh, 'Tell them what they need to know, when they need to know it.' Fortunately I suffered no such restriction. John Gunn and Sadie Stevens bravely made constructive criticisms. Wendy

Acknowledgments

Smith lifted the text with sympathetic editing and pertinent advice. Dean Rockett proofread the manuscript, created the index and was generous with advice, as was Susan Grossman. Lee Send, Roger Lovell and Paul Stevens preserved the text during computer crises. My publishers, Authors On Line Ltd, could not have been more helpful. Nothing has been too much trouble for them.

I have been sustained by the continued interest of Sue Attridge, Iain Barnes, John Gunn, Jane Smith, Sadie Stevens, those members of the Society for Nautical Research (South) unfortunate enough to sit next to me at lunch, fellow students at Birkbeck and the Mary Ward Centre, and by the individual and collective wisdom of Diggers past and present – Peter Ardern, Richard Brooks, Ann Coats, Chris Donnithorne, Val Fontana, Victoria Woodman, Norman Gordon, Trish Lovell, Wendy Smith, Deryck Swetnam, Peter Webberley and Anne Wellsted.

Thank you all.

Introduction

William Knighton is remembered as the indispensable confidant whom George IV trusted to act with efficiency and discretion in matters personal and constitutional, great and small. Between 1822 and 1830 Knighton was a national figure, the intermediary between George and most of the world, but his life at Court was a second career undertaken in early middle age. He was born a farmer's son, came of age in the last quarter of the eighteenth century, and for most of his working life earned his living as a doctor. As a physician Knighton was tied to the eighteenth century, skilled at diagnosis and prognosis but with only limited remedies to hand. As a courtier in the 1820s he served a monarch whose subjects feared revolution but favoured religious tolerance and the reform of public life, and in both careers he moved among larger-than-life characters. During his working life he witnessed the indiscretions of an age in which courtesans and mistresses held power, while retirement gave him leisure to despair of an England that had enacted the Great Electoral Reform Bill. He has much to offer historians. A confirmed landlubber who fled Plymouth to become obstetrician to London society, he was also the Everyman of maritime England who accepted ships and the sea as part of everyday life. His mother was a triumphant example of the advantages of business sense over gentility for Georgian women, while his discriminate exercise of patronage shows its acceptable use in the absence of alternatives.

Yet a study of Knighton's life is more than a reflection of late Georgian England. He was not defined by the age in which he lived. The victories at Trafalgar and Waterloo, the insanity of one king and the extravagance of another, hard harvests, religious dissent and electoral reform were merely context. Knighton's life was shaped by family secrets, a good marriage, a child's death and a capricious employer – common experiences in every society and every age. His life was also shaped by his abilities. A fine intellect and capacity for hard work ensured success at whatever he

Introduction

attempted, but he lacked the spark of genius that would take him to the top of any one career or make it inevitable that he would follow one calling rather than another. With ambition and ability but no vocation, Knighton's life was a series of choices. Some he made wisely. Others he was honest enough to regret.

Who's Who
Same name, different person

William Knighton had many relatives with identical names, and the potential for confusion is especially great in the early chapters. This book therefore allots an alias to eponymous individuals. Whenever possible the alias is a name used by the family. Of the five William Knightons:

	Born as	**Who is he**	**Alias in this book**
1	William Knighton ?c1716–1784	Father of 2 Paternal grandfather of 3	grandfather Knighton
2	William Knighton c1738–1780	Father of 3 Son of 1 First husband of 6	Knighton's father
3	William Knighton c1777–1836	Subject of this biography	Knighton
4	William Knighton 1801–1802	First son of 3 and 7 Died in infancy	Knighton's first-born son
5	William Wellesley Knighton 1811–1885	Surviving son of 3 and 7	William

Of the three Dorothea Knightons:

	Born as	aka	Who is she	Alias in this book
6	Dorothy Hill c1752–1820	[Mrs] Dorothy Knighton [Mrs] Dorothea Knighton [Mrs] Dorothy Toll	Wife of 2 Mother of 3	Dorothy
7	Dorothea Hawker c1780–1862	[Mrs] Dorothea Knighton Lady Knighton	Wife of 3 Mother of 4, 5 and 8	Dorothea
8	Dorothea Knighton 1807–1875	Dora Knighton [Mrs] Dora Seymour [Mrs] Dorothea Seymour	Eldest daughter of 3 and 7 Sister of 5 Wife of 11 Mother of 9	Dora

Of the two Dora Seymours

	Born as	aka	Who is she	Alias in this book
8	Dorothea Knighton 1807–1875	Dora Knighton [Mrs] Dora Seymour [Mrs] Dorothea Seymour	Eldest daughter of 3 and 7 Sister of 5 Wife of 11 Mother of 9	Dora
9	Dorothea Seymour 1830–1901	Dora Seymour	Eldest daughter of 8 and 11 First grandchild of 3 and 7	Little Dora

Introduction

Of the two Michael Seymours:

	Born as	**aka**	**Who is he**	**Alias in this book**
10	Michael Seymour 1768–1834	Captain Seymour Captain Sir Michael Seymour Rear-Admiral Sir Michael Seymour	Husband of Dorothea's sister, Jane Father of 11	Seymour
11	Michael Seymour 1802–1887	Captain Seymour	Son of 10 and Jane Husband of 8	Michael

Same person, different name

Many people associated with Knighton were known by different titles at different times of their lives. On their first appearance in the book they are introduced by the names given to them at birth or marriage together with their most well-known titles. Thereafter they are called by their surnames, with relatives distinguished from each other by the addition of forenames. The ones to remember are:

> RICHARD WELLESLEY, Marquess Wellesley. Richard Wellesley introduced Knighton to the royal household.
> ARTHUR WELLESLEY, Duke of Wellington. Arthur Wellesley was one of Richard Wellesley's younger brothers.
> ROBERT BANKS JENKINSON, Lord Liverpool. Jenkinson was Prime Minister during most of Knighton's years at Court.
> JOHN SCOTT, the Lord Chancellor, styled Lord Eldon.
> FREDERICK JOHN ROBINSON, Lord Goderich. Robinson was Prime Minister for a short time towards the end of George's reign.

George IV (1762–1830) and his brothers

George was the eldest son of George III (1738–1820) and Queen Charlotte (1744–1818), and as the monarch's eldest son and heir to the throne he was initially styled Prince of Wales. Between 1811 and 1820, when his father was incapacitated by illness, he became Prince Regent with limited and then full powers to act as King. On his father's death in 1820 he became George IV. For simplicity this book refers to him as 'George' although his contemporaries did not of course address him by his first name. George's brothers are called by their titles. In this book the most important are:

> FREDERICK, Duke of York. Nearest in age to George, York would have succeeded George as King had he not predeceased him.
>
> WILLIAM, Duke of Clarence, second in line to the throne, became William IV after George's death.
>
> ERNEST, Duke of Cumberland, lived on the Continent for most of George's reign, as did
>
> ADOLPHUS, Duke of Cambridge.

Sources

This is a straightforward account of one man's life, and its readers will be more than capable of checking its veracity without academic referencing. Much of the information came from well-known official sources such as parish records, wills and land tax. Reference books such as the *Oxford Dictionary of National Biography* provided background information. Sources are given in the body of the text or can be identified from the bibliography. With two exceptions references can be found on the websites of institutions that hold the original documents or through The National Archives website. The two exceptions are Knighton's original diary at the Royal Archives, and entries for his London homes in the Middlesex Deeds Registry at Westminster City Archives, both of which are given below.

The *Memoirs*

The starting point for information about Knighton is *Memoirs of Sir William Knighton, Bart, GCH, Keeper of the Privy Purse during the Reign of His Majesty King George the Fourth. Including his correspondence with*

Introduction

many distinguished persons. It is an epistolary biography of correspondence and journal extracts linked by brief narrative passages by his wife, Dorothea, who commenced it with his approval and published it after his death. It was written for Knighton's contemporaries, not for posterity. It is indexed. This book refers to it as the *Memoirs*.

Aspinall's *Letters*

This refers to two series of letters from the Royal Archives and elsewhere edited by Professor Arthur Aspinall of Reading University. The series were not published in chronological order. *Letters of King George IV, 1812–1830* was published in 1938. *Correspondence of George, Prince of Wales, 1770–1810* was published between 1963 and 1971. It includes correspondence that was written after 1810 but which was not available until after the publication of George's correspondence as Regent and King. Both series comprise multiple volumes arranged in date order and are comprehensively indexed.

Knighton's original diary for February 1830

This is a section of Knighton's diary from 1 to 21 February 1830 held at the Royal Archives, Windsor, reference GEO/MAIN/51366–51375, which is cited by kind permission of Her Majesty Queen Elizabeth II. It is part of a bound volume of Knighton's papers at the Royal Archives, reference GEO/MAIN/51247–51382.

Parts of GEO/MAIN/51366–51375 appear in both Aspinall's *Letters* (Nos 1574–1578) and the *Memoirs* (Volume II, pages 101–104). Aspinall's *Letters* contain in full the entries concerning Knighton's public life and omit those concerning his private life. The *Memoirs* omitted Knighton's confidential discussions, his candid observations on people and events, routine details of his life and references to members of his extended family. This book cites Aspinall's *Letters* for Knighton's public life and GEO/MAIN/51366–51375 for his private life.

Middlesex Deeds Registry

This is held at the London Metropolitan Archives and contains abstracts of deeds for properties in the London area. It cannot yet be searched online and some deeds were not registered until several years after their execution. The references for Knighton's London houses are:

28 Argyll Street	MDR 1804/2/351
	MDR 1804/8/84
9 Hanover Square	MDR 1834/8/247
	MDR 1834/8/248
14 Stratford Place	MDR 1834/7/277
	MDR 1836/6/446

Something missing?

Rumours about Knighton started during his lifetime, persisted after his death, and are now too well known to be omitted from his biography. However there are so many that they confuse rather than clarify. This book therefore omits from the main narrative most of the popular myths, mistakes and discrepancies. Instead it draws them together in Chapter 10 and compares them with each other and with disinterested sources to separate fact from faction.

Chapter 1
1777–1797: The Farmer's Son

When William Knighton was in his early twenties he confided to a friend that he knew little about his background. His only certainty was, he wrote, that from his childhood he had been obliged to think, and after two decades of reflection he had pieced together a personal history whose truth he never subsequently questioned. He believed that his father had been a wastrel who, having forfeited hopes of inheriting the main family property, used the proceeds of a nevertheless 'comfortable independence' to drink himself to death by the age of twenty-nine leaving a destitute widow with two children under two. Knighton's conclusions are interesting for two reasons. First, and more importantly, they impelled him as boy, youth and adult, to rise above his father's supposed shame, to become worthy of respect and to achieve financial security. Secondly, they were less than accurate.

Knighton's birthplace, the parish of Bere Ferrers in Devon, is a small inland peninsula created by the rivers Tamar and Tavy as they converge and flow south towards Plymouth. Only the north of the parish has direct contact with the mainland. In Knighton's day there was one bridge and one ford. Otherwise communication was by water. Of its two settlements, Bere Ferrers contained the parish church of St Andrew, while Bere Alston was a rotten borough represented by two Members of Parliament. The land supported arable farming, orchards and, intermittently, the mining of tin, silver and lead. The more prosperous inhabitants were yeomen who lived in homesteads and farmed a mixture of freehold and leasehold land. They emerge from the eighteenth-century parish accounts as literate, capable men, not too proud to claim a shilling or so from the parish funds for killing vermin should an unfortunate badger or otter cross their paths and not afraid to make a fine flourish of a signature. Although one might lease a little more land than his neighbours, the accounts portray a group of equals. Knighton was too common a name to assume family ties, but John and then Samuel Knighton were tenants of a farm known as Lockeridge, and Knighton's paternal grandfather owned and farmed the slightly larger or more profitable estate of Frogstreet.

In April 1761, by accident or design, grandfather Knighton distanced himself from his peers. By then a middle-aged widower with a son and two daughters, he married a younger woman, Elizabeth Jope. Elizabeth would have been nothing more than the daughter of another wealthy yeoman had not her aunt, Frances, married a landed man from Cornwall and died childless. Elizabeth brought to the marriage her father's local estates, a manor in Cornwall and an interest in a country house called Grenofen about six miles north-east of Bere Ferrers at Whitchurch. In addition Elizabeth bore grandfather Knighton two children – Frances Jope Knighton, who was baptised in 1763, and John Moore Knighton, baptised two years later – and it was from the birth of a son to grandfather Knighton by his second wife that speculation dated.

In January 1766 grandfather Knighton bought outright possession of Grenofen. By acquiring a family seat and moving from a homestead to a residence he became a gentleman. A gentleman made provision for his dependents and ensured that his property remained intact and in his family, but grandfather Knighton was a gentleman with two sets of children. His eldest son was a grown man who had been brought up as a farmer, while his youngest son was a child who would know no other life than that of a gentleman. Moreover the young gentleman's mother had made a large financial contribution to the marriage. Grandfather Knighton tackled the problem in two stages. First, in October 1766 he and Elizabeth made a legal settlement of the Cornish property that Elizabeth had brought to the marriage. Secondly, in January 1773 grandfather Knighton made a will to apportion the remainder of the assets that he and Elizabeth possessed. Though generous and devoid of malice, his will was sufficiently unusual to hurt feelings and wound pride.

The English have traditionally bequeathed property by a system called primogeniture, whereby the eldest son inherits the bulk of his father's property so that estates pass down the generations undivided. In the normal course of events Grenofen would have passed to Knighton's father, the only son of grandfather Knighton's first marriage and his elder son by many years, but instead grandfather Knighton willed Grenofen to the young John Moore Knighton, who was to be his only son by Elizabeth. The *Memoirs* insisted that Knighton's father forfeited his inheritance because of 'irregular conduct and an imprudent marriage'. However had he been a teetotal celibate it is by no means certain that he would have inherited Grenofen, for grandfather Knighton and Elizabeth did not bequeath their estates according to the recipients' seniority. The settlement was restricted to Elizabeth's Cornish property and provided for the children of the second marriage. Grandfather Knighton's will apportioned the remainder of the assets and included bequests to the children of his first marriage. Breaking with tradition it treated them equally, and gave Knighton's father no special privileges.

Knighton's father married in October 1772 when he was in his thirties. His bride was Dorothy Hill, aged twenty-one or perhaps twenty, the daughter of a yeoman of similar status to grandfather Knighton, pre-Grenofen. Two-and-a-half centuries later it is hard to understand why marriage to Dorothy was considered imprudent. Knighton's father had been farming at Frogstreet since March 1766, when grandfather Knighton had departed for Grenofen – contrasting signatures on apprenticeship records make it easy to distinguish father from son – and Dorothy was a farmer's daughter. Although the *Memoirs* did not name Dorothy or explain her circumstances, Dorothea described her as 'a person of excellent principles and strong common sense'. To Knighton Dorothy was 'my beloved mother' in life, and 'this pure spirit' in death. The parish register, however, reveals grounds for objection in minds disposed to find them. The bride's signature on the day of her marriage was barely legible and was described for everyone to read as the mark of Dorothy Hill. Grandfather Knighton was not named as a witness, so if father and son had exchanged harsh words it might have seemed to the world that the marriage of Knighton's father and Dorothy

Hill was one irregularity too much for grandfather Knighton. To confirm local suspicions, four months later in January 1773 grandfather Knighton made a will bequeathing not only Grenofen but his Bere Ferrers properties to his younger son, John, under the heading of residuary estate. However he did not forget the children of his first marriage and his will was not the harsh measure that the *Memoirs* implied.

Grandfather Knighton had three surviving children by his first wife. One was Knighton's father. Another was Mary, who was married to William Bredall, a respected surgeon-apothecary at nearby Tavistock. A third, Elizabeth, was married to a yeoman from Ashcombe near Dawlish in east Devon. To each of them, grandfather Knighton bequeathed £1,000. The terms of each bequest were slightly different, but no recipient had direct access to the money and no bequest would benefit a spouse or any descendant more distant than a grandchild. Although John Moore Knighton would become his father's executor when he was twenty-one, the £1,000 bequests were to be administered by separate trustees, sparing the older children the humiliation of having to ask their younger half-brother for money.

Elizabeth had least control over her inheritance, which would go directly to the education and maintenance of her children at the discretion of her trustees, who were William Bredall and an associate of grandfather Knighton named Richard Turner. Knighton's father would inherit under more generous terms. He was exempt from repaying any debts to his father, including debts not yet incurred, and though the latter might be legalese it belies the deep rift described in the *Memoirs*. Knighton's father's share was to be invested with his consent by Bredall and Turner and he would receive the interest. After his death Bredall and Turner would use the money for the maintenance and education of his children. Mary would inherit her £1,000 under the same conditions as Knighton's father. Her trustees, however, would be Turner and Knighton's father. The will that supposedly disinherited Knighton's father for irresponsibility entrusted him with his sister's legacy. Disagreements there may have been, but estrangement existed only in the pages of the *Memoirs*. As the only son of the first marriage Knighton's father might have expected to inherit Frogstreet, but he nevertheless farmed there as grandfather Knighton's tenant, and on the death of Samuel Knighton in September 1777 he took over Lockeridge as well.

In 1780 Knighton's father died, and it is an unquestioned tenet of Knighton's life that the widow and two young children were left destitute by the father's improvidence. In the *Memoirs*, both Knighton's letters and Dorothea's narrative divided the family into good people and bad people, with Dorothy and grandfather Knighton in the first category, and Knighton's father and uncle John Moore Knighton in the second. The case against Knighton's father is far from proven. The *Memoirs* stated that he died at the age of twenty-nine having 'spent in irregularity and intemperance a comfortable independence' and leaving an impoverished widow and two children. Knighton admitted that he knew little about his own early childhood, but his ignorance was greater than he realised. The *Memoirs* gave Knighton's father an approximate birth date of 1750, but Bere Ferrers' parish registers suggest that he was baptised in 1738, while a handwritten note on a local survey describes him as being thirty-five in 1774. He died in July 1780 in his early forties, a respectable age for a man in late eighteenth-century Bere Ferrers, as a tenant of both Frogstreet and Lockeridge. Moreover between 1777 and 1778 the elegant 'William' of his signature unaccountably contracted to 'Wiam', suggesting that for the last years of his life he was not drunken but ill.

Knighton was equally mistaken about the timing of his father's death, believing that it occurred before 'the sun had shone two years on one [child, Knighton] and one year on the other [child, Thamzin]'. True, Knighton's father died in July 1780, nine months after Thamzin's baptism. However Knighton was baptised in January 1777, so he was at least three-and-a-half when his father died. Knighton's tale of the destitute young wife whose two babes barely escaped the care of the parish was also unreliable, as was his account of grandfather Knighton's death occurring immediately after that of Knighton's father. Grandfather Knighton died in 1784, while the land tax assessment and parish accounts for 1781 show Dorothy at Frogstreet and then at Lockeridge, where she stayed for the rest of her working life. For reasons unknown this simple chronology was concealed from both Knighton the child, who could only listen, observe and surmise, and from Knighton the adult, who became determined to rise above his father's alleged shame.

Knighton recalled that he spent his infancy not at Lockeridge but 'in an abode of a very superior description'. He and Thamzin were perhaps removed to Grenofen after their father's death, for grandfather Knighton proceeded to make a landowner out of his infant grandson. From May 1781, nearly a year after the death of Knighton's father, a 'William Knighton Junr' or 'William Knighton' appeared on the land tax assessment as the proprietor of land let to a tenant and liable to £1 tax. This William Knighton was an entirely separate proprietor from grandfather Knighton, who was 'William Knighton Esq'. Subsequent entries identify the land as three plots assessed at 6s 8d each – Luxes Park, Bayleys and Ashdon. Meanwhile in April 1782 Dorothy married James Toll, a man of around her own age from a similar yeoman background, signing the parish register in a clear, confident hand, and by the time Knighton was five or six he was at Lockeridge. The *Memoirs* omitted any details that might identify James Toll but made it clear that he was a fair man who did not discriminate against his stepchildren. The only other information about him is equally appealing – either James or his father played cello in the church orchestra. James Toll died in March 1790 aged only thirty-seven. The marriage produced four children of whom two boys and a girl survived to adulthood. Knighton remained close to at least one – John, the younger of his two half-brothers. However the *Memoirs*' only reference to the early 1780s was an anecdote about Knighton, aged about six, dressing up as a clergyman in Dorothy's white apron, standing on a chair in the farmhouse kitchen and haranguing her domestics because he thought that he could 'improve' them. Somewhere, somehow, he had picked up the notion that being good was vital.

1777–1797: The Farmer's Son

Grandfather Knighton's £1,000 provided the means for self-improvement. Thamzin received the education that her mother had been denied, and Knighton later teased her about reading romances. For boys there were grammar schools at Plymouth and Plympton, but Knighton, at the age of around twelve, was sent to a small boarding school at Newton Bushell in east Devon. According to his own account he spent more than four years there without much benefit, but Dorothea was more kindly disposed towards it. The family's plans for Knighton required the school to make him numerate and literate and give him a good knowledge of Latin, and that is what it did.

Although Knighton detested his uncle, John Moore Knighton, the son of grandfather Knighton's second marriage, he was close to Frances, the daughter of that marriage. As a young man he corresponded with her, and in later life he named his second daughter Mary Frances, combining the names of two of his three paternal aunts. In September 1793 Knighton was apprenticed to William Bredall, Mary's husband and the second of four generations of Tavistock medical men, for a premium of £132. If there was ever prejudice against Dorothy it died with grandfather Knighton, and there is no hint that Knighton was discouraged from seeing her. Apprentices usually lived with their masters, and Knighton later wrote that his walk at six in the morning was along the banks of the Tavy as far as Crowndale, the birthplace of Sir Francis Drake, which would fit a walk from Tavistock in the direction of Bere Ferrers on a day off.

As a surgeon-apothecary William Bredall made and prescribed medicine, set bones, delivered children and performed whatever surgery was within his competence. Although Knighton subsequently trained in London and Edinburgh, it was Bredall's methods that he admired throughout his life and which were the basis for the wide practical knowledge for which he became known. Bredall had a large practice of both private and institutional patients, and a pamphlet that Knighton published in 1800 described Bredall treating troops stationed at Tavistock. Equally important was the way in which Bredall conducted his practice. The accounts of Bere Ferrers' parish overseers include Bredall's bill for the year October 1794 to October 1795. The bill reveals nothing of Bredall's methods or medicines, making no distinction between one bottle of gargle and the next. It does, however, include journeys and attendances for which Bredall made no charge. He let it be known that he was a gentleman capable of acts of goodwill, not a tradesman working at a fixed rate.

While Knighton was an apprentice he endeavoured to keep up the Greek and Latin that he had learned at Newton Bushell and to improve his general knowledge. When he was sixteen an elderly schoolmaster lent him a book of poetry by Alexander Pope, whose pithy, economic observations of men and manners, divorced from their rhyming pentameters, live on in everyday speech – more than two-and-a-half centuries after Pope's death we have yet to improve on 'Damn with faint praise'. Knighton read the book so avidly on his morning walks that he remembered it whole. However his delight at the depth and subtlety that Pope could convey in so few words was diminished by the realisation that he had left school before he became aware of Pope's existence. Using money set aside for a new suit of clothes he bought a book. However it was not his own copy of Pope but the now untraceable *Winterbottom's History of America*. What Knighton called his 'project' was to see America. He was no angry young man who rejected his family, but somewhere in his mind was the possibility of escape from Devon and its associations and from the limitations of his education.

Despite bad feeling between Knighton and John Moore Knighton, John's sister, Frances, treated Knighton with kindness. In February 1793, seven months before Knighton was apprenticed to Bredall, France declared war on Britain and, while the standing army was fighting abroad, a part-time army of volunteer corps and militias defended the home country from invasion and insurrection. Militia officers were the fine body of men whose dashing red coats caused such a stir among the females of Jane Austen's novels, and many volunteer corps' uniforms were equally flattering. In November 1795 Frances's husband, then a major in the Tavistock Volunteer Corps, obtained for Knighton a commission as second lieutenant. Knighton's volunteer service probably cost him more than he received in pay and allowances, but it was not without reward. First, even the most junior commission helped a young man become a gentleman. Secondly, volunteers were exempt from militia service, which was otherwise avoidable only by taking out insurance, paying a fine or finding a substitute. Exemption meant that Knighton would not fall under the command of John Moore Knighton, who was an officer in the local militia. In addition, as a volunteer rather than a militiaman, Knighton would not be sent out of the county and could continue his apprenticeship.

While Knighton was apprenticed to Bredall he made two important professional contacts. One was Stephen Hammick, a man of his own age who was training at the Royal Naval Hospital at Plymouth. The other was Dr Francis Geach, the Royal's senior surgeon, whom John Wesley described as a man of sense and learning. Geach, who was approaching his seventies, ultimately hampered Knighton's medical career by encouraging him to disdain the scientific medical community, but it was thanks to Geach that Knighton established himself as a doctor. Although the *Memoirs* skimped this phase of Knighton's life, the research of medical historian Susan Lawrence, who studied the records of hundreds of medical students, makes sense of passing references. While Knighton was still with Bredall, Geach set him to writing up case notes, for perusal of case notes by an experienced physician was the only form of on-going assessment available. Recorded observations were the standard way of writing about medicine in contemporary publications, and the naming of body parts in case notes was becoming more precise. To be accepted by his medical contemporaries a man had to express himself in the same terms. Bredall's practice would pass to his son and Knighton would have to find his own place in his profession.

A rite of passage for young provincial medical men who, like Knighton, had completed most of their training but had yet to start in practice was to spend six months 'walking the wards' at a London hospital, attending lectures and dissecting. Generations of students made the same comments – that not all the methods they learnt were better than those they had been taught, and that they were unlikely to need all the training they received in London for the practices to which they would return, for many were destined to take over a father's patients. They did, however, learn to comport themselves as gentlemen and professionals. In September 1796, funded by his inheritance, Knighton enrolled at St Thomas's. The *Memoirs* described this part of Knighton's life by means of his letters home to his sister, friends and mentors. There are no surviving letters to Dorothy, who perhaps never became sufficiently literate to feel comfortable receiving letters, but Thamzin passed on affectionate messages between mother and son. Knighton's descriptions of his life in London are corroborated by the research of Susan Lawrence and by the published letters of medical student Hampton Weekes. Weekes attended St Thomas's five years after Knighton, starting in September 1801 and leaving the following January, and his letters home are published in their entirety.

Guy's and St Thomas's hospitals were on the south bank of the Thames where Borough High Street approaches London Bridge, and were separated only by St Thomas's Street. Students from one establishment could study at the other, with St Thomas's specialising in surgery and Guy's in medicine, also known as 'physic'. Students paid fees to a senior physician or surgeon and, according to how much they paid, would simply walk the wards or become involved in their medical man's work. Although Knighton later developed a preference for physic, the archives of King's College, London show that on 29 September 1796 he paid £25 4s to become a pupil of Henry Cline, a prestigious surgeon whom he later encountered in the royal household. In 1796, however, Knighton was among the students who walked the wards with the great man, aware of the money laid out on their behalf and anxious not to miss a word.

As professional men, pupils had to live like gentlemen. Weekes gave some of his clothing to a servant in lieu of a Christmas box and accepted an invitation to a dance for which he had to buy dancing shoes and silk breeches. Knighton, lacking advice and bedevilled by earnestness, declined a professionally advantageous invitation to dine rather than fall behind with his studies. Living in London entailed new practical arrangements about which we know nothing. How did Knighton receive his money? Did he lodge with a family, all-in, or did he take a room and cater for himself? When he was hungry between meals did he, like Weekes, buy himself 6d worth of oysters? Medical students in London were young men in their late teens or early twenties who had spent the past few years in long hours of physically active work. Food treats were noteworthy events for Weekes, who welcomed the appearance at breakfast of hot rolls instead of the usual dry toast and received fruit and the occasional hare from his family. Using Weekes as a model, Knighton's six months in London cost perhaps £150 or so in travel and porterage, course fees, board and lodging, laundry, medical books and instruments, and the paper on which to write – a significant expense compared with today's factory-produced reams of A4. Grandfather Knighton's bequest was laid out at interest, but Knighton's education was depleting his share and had to result in a viable career.

Knighton's letters to Devon described a full day's study from morning to late evening, walking the wards, attending lectures and dissecting, with many hours transcribing his notes afterwards. The accounts of other students corroborate his experience. Lectures in different aspects of medicine were available independently of the hospitals but were designed to fit in with the pupils' hospital studies. They cost £3 to £4 a course, and Knighton attended anatomy, midwifery, physic and surgery, the last under Astley Cooper, another medical man whom he later met in the royal household. It was common for students to visit other medical institutions on their own initiative, and Knighton visited Bedlam. Where he differed from his contemporaries was his lack of excitement at the new knowledge. He admired the conduct of operations at St Thomas's but for physic remained influenced by Geach who in turn looked to Plymouth physician John Huxham, an internationally-acclaimed expert on fever and diphtheria, but born at the end of the seventeenth century. As a result Knighton placed little value on the practice of physic taught at Guy's, though he did not explain how it differed from what he had been taught or why he disliked it. While Knighton was in London both Geach and Bredall apparently failed to give him specific instructions. His letters to them from London contained only general observations, unsupported opinion and poetry. His preference for familiar methods seemed based on loyalty to people to whom he owed a debt of gratitude. Lacking supervision, he set himself on a treadmill of note-taking and transcription as though sheer effort would see him through. In contrast Weekes sent his written-up notes for assessment by his father, who told him not to bother recording information he already knew and specifying aspects where Weekes should especially note London methods.

All students found dissection a revelation and believed it the best way of understanding anatomy. Weekes' letters described the practical difficulties. The dissection room was of necessity cold, so students were advised to dress warmly in flannels and if necessary drink a little brandy or porter – a strong beer – which would guard against cold and nausea. Students wore special clothing to dissect – Weekes described a dark brown gown and sleeves or, cheaper but decidedly inferior in his view, a sort of pinafore of dark brown Holland, a coarse linen also used for furnishings. Students inevitably cut their fingers dissecting, with the risk that the wound would become infected from the cadaver, so they were told to eat well and keep healthy.

The danger was far from theoretical. Students and medical practitioners from St Thomas's and Guy's were eligible to join Guy's Physical Society which met each Saturday night from October to May in the operating theatre at Guy's and, under the chairmanship of a senior medical man, heard papers or discussed case notes. An earnest body, which made no exception for Christmas and New Year's Eves, it fined members deemed absent without good reason and used the income to buy books for its library. At Geach's suggestion Knighton joined, though the advice was belated and Knighton was not elected until 12 November, the seventh meeting of the session. Five weeks later the speaker was a fellow student, Hall Overend from Sheffield. Overend read case notes that he had made not as a medical practitioner but as a patient, describing the danger, uncertainty and sheer unpleasantness for both patient and practitioner in the late eighteenth century. On Friday, 14 October Overend had scratched his finger in the dissecting room but, believing the wound too insignificant to need attention, ignored it. By Sunday night, however, the cut was ulcerated and painful, his whole arm was stiff and he had a swollen gland in his armpit. Overend healed the wound but the pain and swelling increased and the following weekend he consulted Cooper. During the next two weeks Overend deteriorated quickly, suffering throbbing pain, delirium and debility. The swelling hardened and filled his armpit, at one stage extending to his nipple. Cooper prescribed leeches and a succession of purgatives to flush out the infection, and opium for the pain, with repeated incisions to remove pus from the swelling, and recommended a simple diet with no alcohol. At the time of speaking Overend was greatly although not completely recovered.

Whereas Overend held the floor for a whole meeting, Knighton spoke only once, on 21 January 1797, to second the election of a fellow student. However if Knighton lacked the confidence to draw attention to himself in London, Geach had been active on his behalf in Plymouth. On Saturday, 28 January Knighton was for the first time marked absent and finable. The following Thursday he was one of thirty-eight men who appeared before the Company of Surgeons' Court of Examiners in the anatomy theatre of Surgeons' Hall, next to Newgate Prison in the Old Bailey, near St Paul's. Two sought superannuation on the grounds of age and ill health. The remainder undertook an oral examination to allow them to work as surgeons, mostly in the armed services. One failed. Two were approved as hospital mates. Knighton was among only four to be awarded a diploma – as surgeons were not required to attend a university they could not receive a degree. In addition he was approved as assistant surgeon at Plymouth Hospital. The *Memoirs* omitted the episode, but naval surgeon Peter Cullen, who took his examination nearly seven years earlier, found the bureaucracy sufficiently disconcerting to record it in his journal. Recommended for a post as assistant surgeon on board the frigate *Squirrel*, Cullen went to the Navy Office at Somerset House in the Strand and was given an order enabling him to be examined as an assistant surgeon in the navy at the next fortnightly examination at Surgeons' Hall. Examinations were held at night, and Cullen arrived at seven o'clock. Two or more candidates were examined simultaneously, standing in front of a semi-circular table around which were seated the examiners with the president in the centre. Cullen successfully answered questions on anatomy, physiology, and the treatment of different surgical cases, after which his examiner introduced him to the president, who bowed, asked him to pay a guinea, and told him to collect his certificate from the Navy Office the next day. The advice was wrong. A certificate proved only that the candidate had qualified as a naval surgeon, and it stayed at the Navy Office. To take up his post Cullen needed a warrant, but the Navy Office would not issue a warrant until the *Squirrel*'s captain formally applied for him. Cullen waited anxiously, fearing that he might literally miss the boat, but the Navy Office at last received a formal application, and on payment of a further guinea issued him with a warrant.

If Knighton encountered similar difficulties, he overcame them. At the Physical Society meeting of Saturday, 4 February he was again marked absent and finable, and at the next meeting it was reported that he wished to be considered as a corresponding member. He had left London.

Chapter 2
1797–1809: The Young Doctor

A recurrent feature of war with France was the presence of Royal Navy ships around France's most western coastline to prevent the French navy from leaving its port at Brest on the Atlantic coast. In December 1796, while Knighton was walking the wards, British watch over Brest had increased with the Channel Fleet at sea in wet and wintry locations. Despite improvements in naval hygiene, to remain static and afloat in a cold, damp climate was unhealthy, and a frequent destination for Channel Fleet casualties was the Royal Naval Hospital at Stonehouse, between the town of Plymouth and Plymouth Dockyard. On 8 January 1797 William Farr, senior physician at the Royal Naval Hospital, warned Governor Richard Creyke of the emergency created by a sudden increase in the number of patients, and the next day he reported that new Admiralty instructions on storekeeping had created extra work.

The crisis brought opportunities for young medical men. On 15 January Creyke recommended to the Royal Navy's Sick and Wounded Board that nineteen-year-old Stephen Hammick, who had worked at the hospital for nearly five years and was by then assistant surgeon, be promoted to upper assistant surgeon. In the same letter Creyke requested a new assistant surgeon to replace Hammick, and on 14 February received 'Mr Wm. Knighton', whose absence from Guy's Physical Society had been noted only two weeks earlier. Knighton later maintained that his time with Geach was dedicated to professional improvement, not mercenary gain, but in reality it offered him experience and financial respite. The Royal was built in an innovative system of isolated blocks to limit the spread of infection, and in 1797 it was barely thirty-five years old. Knighton shared Geach's accommodation there, and his drugs and instruments were provided. He was initially paid four shillings a day, and in May he asked for an increase and received a further one shilling a day.

Sir William Knighton

The duties of surgeons and physicians at naval hospitals were described in *The Naval Surgeon* by William Turnbull, published in 1806. The injuries they saw had already been identified on board by ships' surgeons who had stopped the bleeding and given initial treatment. Turnbull also identified specific diseases of the Channel duties – smallpox, fevers, agues, inflammations, catarrhal infections, consumption, scurvy and venereal disease. Typhus, transmitted by lice and also known as gaol-fever, was especially prevalent in winter because of cold and overcrowding, as was dysentery. Most of the patients listed in the Royal's muster books had rheumatism, fever or venereal ulcers; only a minority of Knighton's patients were hospitalised because of wounds. He was allowed to operate, and he had an authority over his naval patients that he would not have with his private patients, but he did not have to enforce hospital discipline. Creyke dealt with everything from allegations of malpractice to nurses who brought alcohol in and candles out. A humane and pragmatic man, he declined to discipline a marine who had plotted with another patient to rub arsenic into their skin so that they would get sores and be invalided out. As Creyke noted, the marine was already dying from his previous attempts to obtain a medical discharge.

The Royal was a microcosm of Plymouth society. Knighton might have been distantly related to its chaplain, the Reverend George Jope. He became a friend and admirer of Stephen Hammick who was soon recognised as a gifted surgeon. The Royal's dispenser was Hammick's father, an alderman with a private practice as a surgeon who had nevertheless trained his son at the Royal's dispensary. The assistant dispenser was Jacob Hawker, son of the clergyman who would console Knighton on the death of his baby son in 1802. Other assistant surgeons included Samuel Fuge, who was, or who was related to, a founder member of the Plymouth Medical Society, and Nathaniel Seccombe, who additionally worked at Plymouth's civilian dispensary. Knighton also made social contacts. Samuel Northcote, the Royal's clockmaker, was brother to artist James, who became a neighbour of Knighton and his future wife in London and remained their friend until his death thirty years later. Lieutenant Richard Seymour, admitted in haste as a patient in September 1797, became a brother-in-law.

The Royal's doctors were supposed to limit their private practices, but suitable staff were scarce and the regulation was not enforced. Geach had built up a large private practice. His mentor, Huxham, had shamelessly brought himself to public notice by ruses that included ostentatious clothing. In the same tradition Geach promised to introduce Knighton to 'life and business' and make his talents known. On Geach's advice Knighton submitted a medical essay to the University of St Andrews and was awarded the equivalent of an honorary Master of Arts degree. The mentor–protégé relationship was mutually beneficial. By April 1797 Geach was, Creyke recorded, too ill to attend his wards. Knighton helped Geach in the hospital and in private practice, and in August 1797 he resigned his volunteer commission.

In February 1798 Geach died. Knighton was forced into independence, but he was no longer the diffident student who could find nothing to say at a meeting of fellow professionals or who would turn down a professionally advantageous invitation so that he could write up his notes. The *Memoirs* referred twice to a legal action that he instituted around this time against his wicked paternal uncle, John Moore Knighton. It concerned what Dorothea described as a small estate purchased by grandfather Knighton and not specifically willed to John Moore Knighton, by which she meant the three plots in Bere Ferrers on which the young Knighton paid land tax and received rent. By 1790 John Moore Knighton had appropriated Ashdon, reducing Knighton to Luxes Park and Bayleys. In 1795 Knighton lost these too, and they appeared as late entries to the land tax schedule, squeezed in under the name of a wealthy local landowner. Despite Dorothea's claim that Knighton was heir-at-law to the estate, John Moore Knighton could reasonably have assumed that it was included in the residuary estate to which he was entitled under grandfather Knighton's will. Nevertheless it was unnecessary for two men who between them owned swathes of Devon and Cornwall to filch a couple of fields from a young man without connections who was endeavouring to make himself independent, and it was unwise to filch them from a young man who had been mentored by Geach. Between 1798 and 1799 Luxes Park and Bayleys were restored to Knighton. Becoming collectively known as Luxes Park, they remained in his possession until his death and then passed to his son.

It is impossible to calculate how much rent Knighton received from Luxes Park. We can only compare his £1 tax liability with the £2 14s or so payable on each of the homesteads of Frogstreet and Lockeridge. Whatever the details, in the summer of 1798 Knighton was in private practice at 43 George Street, a small terraced house in what Dorothea called 'the best part of Devonport', and in November 1798, described as a surgeon, he received £150 to take one Benjamin Ramsey as an apprentice. Plymouth Dock, also called Dock, was the area now known as Devonport and had grown around Plymouth Dockyard as a distinct town, separate from Plymouth. It was by and large pleasant and cultured, with circulating libraries, theatre and assembly room, and its hilly site overlooked the sea. However it was not convenient for duties at the Royal. Sandwiched between the Dockyard and barracks, surrounded by a wall and defended from attack on its landward side by unbroken earthen fortifications, Dock was in addition separated from the Royal by Stonehouse Creek. Knighton left the Royal on amicable terms in September 1799.

According to Hammick's obituary, much of Knighton's early professional employment was the result of their friendship. The *Memoirs* recalled that Knighton attended respectable families in both the town and the surrounding countryside, together with military, naval and other visitors to the area, but we know little about how he ran his practice. He believed that because he needed only four hours' sleep a night he gained time that others lost, so he may simply have been more accessible than his competitors. On one particular day, which he described as 'long and tedious', he saw between fifty and sixty patients, and simple arithmetic suggests that he was also visiting doctor to an institution where patients came in batches. Doctors were 'to be found' at their addresses but attended patients in their own homes. Although Knighton was never a confident horseman, he probably rode to his more remote patients, as Geach did.

Despite his thriving practice, Knighton did not perceive his competence as limited to medicine, and while attending the president of the Board of Agriculture he wondered whether he should impress his patient by putting together an essay on the use of salt in farming. Knighton needed to become known outside Plymouth. The sight of Dorothy selling her produce from Lockeridge at Plymouth market was a gift to gossips, and Knighton described the stories told of him as 'beyond everything wonderful'. Dorothea wrote that he had to overcome 'ill-founded reports of disqualification, inexperience, &c.', and a fellow doctor tried to discredit him. Repeated apologies and an invitation to dine only increased Knighton's suspicion but an old friend, Alexander Pope, provided support. Pope had understood an outsider's vulnerability because he had been a cripple and a Roman Catholic. In 1688, the year of Pope's birth, England had exchanged James II, a Roman Catholic, for William III, a Protestant, and the nation's subsequent fear of James' descendants, the Jacobites, meant that Roman Catholics could not hold Government posts or attend universities. All Roman Catholics were objects of suspicion. Pope survived by publishing his wit, and his poetry still echoes the experience of everyone who has suffered prejudice and jealousy. Knighton quoted Pope's question, 'Say, is their anger or their friendship worse?' to describe the duplicity of his fellow practitioners in Plymouth, and the observation, 'It is the slaver kills, and not the bite' to describe their mental state.

The most influential local medical practitioners formed the Plymouth Medical Society, an invitation-only lunar club whose members met at each other's houses at seven o'clock on the Friday evening nearest the full moon so as to have all possible light for their journeys. Knighton was not a member. He believed that his fellow professionals were jealous that he had inherited Geach's extensive practice, but he was perhaps tainted by a controversy surrounding Geach. Geach was beloved of the naval men he treated and respected by his private clients, but he was not universally popular with his fellow physicians. In the 1760s Huxham had sought to enhance Geach's reputation by submitting some of Geach's surgical cases for publication by the prestigious scientific body, the Royal Society. However the Huxham connection also harmed Geach. Huxham had researched a debilitating regional ailment known as Devon colic, observing that it coincided with the annual production of fresh cider. He attributed the cause to acidity, but another physician built on his work and made the connection between the colic and the lead used in cider presses. In a cider-producing county it was imperative to establish the true cause of the illness, and during the controversy Geach was among the defenders of the ultimately discredited lead press.

In practice as a young doctor and his mentor dead, Knighton looked back to a golden age of medicine as practised by Huxham, and spent his spare time in 'investigation of the ancient physicians'. Although Knighton was described as a surgeon when he practised at George Street, he wrote that he had 'ever felt a peculiar talent for the study of physic' and that he felt at home with it, and in May 1800 he acquired another degree from St Andrews. His new qualification was an MD, or Doctor of Medicine. A St Andrews MD was available on submission of a £20 fee and testimonials from two well-known medical practitioners – Knighton's were Dr Stephen Luke of Falmouth, who had built his reputation treating the invalids who went to Falmouth to embark for warmer climates, and the now unknown Dr Charles Aimsworth, also of Devon. Nevertheless it was a generally accepted qualification. When the Company of Surgeons obtained a new charter and became the Royal College of Surgeons in 1800 Knighton declined the invitation to apply for membership to which he was entitled. Instead, as William Knighton, MD, he published a paper on Geach's and Bredall's method of treating 'putrid fever' with mercury. The printer was from George Street; the distributing bookseller was in London.

In August of the same year, 1800, Knighton married into one of Plymouth's most respected and well-connected families. His wife, Dorothea, was the youngest of five daughters of Captain James Hawker of the Royal

Navy. Hawker had died fourteen years earlier after a career that included service as a revenue officer in North America, and an American naval historian has suggested that with a few more officers such as Hawker the War of Independence might have broken out somewhat earlier. Hawker was nevertheless a brave man and a loyal officer. He was also of independent mind. Unlike many Royal Navy officers, he spent his prize money not on a country seat but on investment property. Further, in an age when, as naval historian Nicholas Rodger points out, promotion to lieutenant instantly transformed a young man into a gentleman, Hawker set up his eldest son as a timber merchant, for it was also a time of war fought in wooden ships by an expanding population whose houses were built of brick and wood and filled with wooden furniture.

Dorothea was only nineteen or twenty at the time of her marriage, so would have needed her mother's consent to marry. To be accepted as good enough for a daughter of James Hawker was an achievement. The Hawkers were linked by marriage to overlapping local networks of politics, land and trade. Sarah, nearest in age to Dorothea, had married into the Luscombes, an influential landowning family. The remaining three sisters were married to Royal Navy officers. Now unknown outside naval history, Charles Boyles, Edward Osborn and Michael Seymour were national heroes to their contemporaries. Dorothea's eldest sister, Mary, brought a dowry of £6,000 to her marriage to Charles Boyles, and Sarah also received a settlement, but if Dorothea received a dowry it was a private family arrangement, for Hawker's will had made no specific provision. Knighton's marriage was beyond all doubt a love match. More than thirty years later Dorothea recalled the grave, handsome young doctor, while Knighton recalled the difficulty of a single man or woman in coming to terms with the 'insulated state' of having no companion in life. He believed that men and women needed each other.

Dorothea was accomplished and well educated. The *Memoirs* mentioned in passing that she had travelled in Europe without Knighton, presumably before their marriage, and his friends and colleagues described her as a woman of intelligence and integrity. Love of art was perhaps common ground during her courtship. Medical note-taking required at least rudimentary sketches and, though Knighton became known as a connoisseur in later life, he also painted for pleasure. George Pycroft, who published in 1883 when people who had known Dorothea were still alive, said that she showed considerable talent from a young age, being skilled at depictions of Devon scenery and portraits, and possessing 'a ready hand for grouping figures' in what Pycroft called '*genre* compositions'. These depicted figures based on living models but arranged by the artist to portray hypothetical views of everyday life, often conveying a story or moral. James Northcote, the Plymouth-born painter who became the Knightons' friend, considered Dorothea talented and encouraged her. Another Devon painter, Samuel Prout, recalled his pleasure on first seeing her paintings. When Prout was incapacitated by headaches he begged a prescription from Knighton, but it was to Dorothea that he offered to show his sketchbook of Italy.

When work took Knighton away from Dorothea he ceaselessly told her how cruelly he missed her, and he unburdened himself to her in a lifetime of letters. He did not, however, treat her as an equal. He acknowledged her practical ability as an artist but implied that he had the finer 'sentiment of feeling', and he once announced a drastic change of residence without first ascertaining her opinion. There was a visit to her mother in the early years of their marriage and anxious enquiries from her extended family. Information about her is scant. Whereas Knighton's evolving character is reflected in his correspondence from youth to late middle age, Dorothea's character must be deduced from her narrative in the *Memoirs*, which she compiled after his death. She was then a newly-bereaved widow in her fifties, possessed of an uncompromising faith that demanded unquestioning resignation to God's will but which guaranteed that God would never refuse an appeal for comfort in the adversity that He inflicted, for He had wise if unfathomable reasons for inflicting it.

Sixteen months after their marriage Knighton and Dorothea suffered an adversity that, before the twentieth century, few parents were spared. In the summer of 1801 they nearly lost their first-born son to convulsions. The baby recovered, only to be taken ill early in 1802. He died on the night of 20 January and was buried three days later at St Andrew's, Bere Ferrers. No two people respond to bereavement in the same way. Knighton toiled on in private practice for another year in a state of unresolved unhappiness that went beyond grief, dissatisfied with everything he had achieved and with everything that he was likely to achieve. Then, miraculously, the fog of misery became a plan. A lifetime in provincial practice was not his inevitable destiny. Telling only a few people, Knighton decided to make a fresh start in London.

The *Memoirs* recorded that Knighton was known to only a few people in London, but that was the appeal. He travelled to London without Dorothea, but she had joined him by November 1803 when the landscape artist Joseph Farington visited her at Princes Street, off Hanover Square. Farington, whose naval cousin had been a Plymouth MP when Knighton was still Bredall's apprentice, knew her not as Dr Knighton's wife but as the former Miss Hawker and sister of Mrs Boyles. In late February 1804 Knighton bought a house in Argyll Street where James Northcote had lived with his sister for many years. The property was No 28, some distance from the junction with Oxford Street and nearly opposite Argyll House, the London home of the Dukes of Argyll. According to the parish rates it had been empty for some time, but it was a prestigious address with an army officer on one side and a baronet's widow on the other.

The purchase was a mistake. To practise as a physician in London Knighton needed to become a Licentiate of the Royal College of Physicians of London. His St Andrews degree was a common qualification held by many distinguished London physicians and he believed that it entitled him to take the College's Licentiate examination. His application was supported by Sir Francis Milman, a royal physician and future president of the College, who recommended Knighton as 'a worthy deserving man, a man of talent and his [Milman's] particular friend'. However Knighton's application was ill timed and the College refused to examine him. Sir George Clark's *History of the Royal College of Physicians of London* does not mention Knighton by name, but it confirms his experience.

While Dorothea was visiting her mother in Devon she received from Knighton a letter in which he complained about an 'oppressive law' that the College was employing against him. Clark explains that in the 1770s the College introduced statutes requiring Licentiates to have studied for two years at a university, although it was not necessary to obtain a degree. A would-be applicant later obtained a King's Bench ruling that the College had a duty to examine everyone who applied but, Clark notes, it appears that no one took advantage of the ruling. Knighton believed that the statute had never been invoked until his application. However, unbeknown to him the College had been mulling over the increased status and autonomy obtained by the surgeons in 1800. In 1804 it suddenly embarked upon plans to reform its profession. Among these was a proposal of June 1804 requiring Licentiates to have a degree from a university in England, Scotland or Ireland obtained after completing a full course of study. The proposal was as yet unenforceable but it indicated what would be expected in future. The College began to summon non-Licentiates who were practising as physicians, and those who were unwilling or unable to be examined were ordered to limit themselves to midwifery and pharmacy.

Having escaped from Devon Knighton would not contemplate return. Neither would he remain in London with his competency in doubt or his practice confined. He explained to Dorothea that they were moving to Edinburgh where he would attend the university and take a medical degree. On his return to London he would be able to demand what he had once solicited, for the College would be compelled by its own statutes to examine him. In a new, confident, self-mocking tone he admitted his pursuit of fame and fortune but reasoned that provided they were acquired through virtue and industry they harmed no one. There was 'always a gap in the hedge that a man may step into' by being better, more industrious and more attentive to detail than his contemporaries. Dorothea's reply does not survive. When she compiled the *Memoirs* more than thirty years later she wrote only that a 'house which had been purchased and furnished in Argyle-street was disposed of'. It is not certain that the Knightons ever lived at No 28. In June 1804 it was empty again, and a newly-decorated town residence in Argyll Street, opposite Argyll House but not identified by number, was advertised in *The Times* on 30 August to be auctioned on 27 September. Although Knighton did not formally sell No 28 until 19 October, on 10 October it was insured by its next owner, Caleb Whitefoord, a wine merchant, diplomat and patron of science and the arts. Knighton almost certainly signed the deeds in advance, for by 10 October he had enrolled at Edinburgh.

For Edinburgh, as for St Thomas's, the *Memoirs* said little, but Lisa Rosner's study describes the common experiences of Edinburgh medical students and confirms the *Memoirs'* account. The easiest journey to Edinburgh was by sea, and students landed at Leith in mid-October so as to be ready when lectures started in the first week of November. The winter session ended in April and, unlike St Thomas's, Edinburgh offered a summer session from May to the end of July. Many students left Edinburgh to work during the summer, and in April 1805 a Sarah Knollis wrote to her father from Bath that an acquaintance had heard that Dr Knighton was in London. If so, he did not remain there, for a letter from Northcote to the Knightons in Edinburgh was dated 28 July 1805. Most students lodged near the university, paying about £16 per person per quarter for a room with breakfast and supper; Knighton and Dorothea lodged with a Mrs McGilvray whom Knighton remembered with affection and whom he tried to find when he visited Edinburgh with George in 1822. Other costs were a small matriculation fee to enrol at the university and lecture fees similar to those in London. Because Edinburgh was a university, not a hospital, students walked the wards at the city's Infirmary. In all other respects the routine of lectures, note-taking and transcription was identical to that at St Thomas's.

Now in his late twenties, Knighton was among a substantial minority of older medical students at Edinburgh. He had spent the intervening years at a modern hospital and in private practice. Married to an educated, intelligent woman, he was no longer alone and unsupported. All diffidence lost, Knighton became one of a group of five friends – the others were Robert Gooch, Edmund Lockyer, Henry Fearon and Henry Southey, whose brother became poet laureate – brought together by pre-existing ties. Gooch, who became a gifted obstetrician and later treated many of Knighton's patients, lodged at the same house as Fearon and Southey. Gooch had known Southey as a boy and while at Edinburgh had become a close friend of Lockyer, who came from Plymouth and whom Knighton perhaps already knew. As students in Edinburgh the men reinforced their friendship and prepared for examinations by conversing in Latin, and they remained close throughout their careers.

Although Knighton had originally intended to take his degree at Edinburgh, in the end he left without a qualification. Lisa Rosner found that that was what most Edinburgh students did, their choice of courses suggesting that they had never intended to take the degree and had attended only to widen their knowledge. Knighton, like many others, applied instead for a degree from King's College, Aberdeen. His application was supported by Lockyer and by Ralph Blegborough, a London obstetrician who encountered various problems with the Royal College of Physicians. Knighton was awarded an Aberdeen MD in April 1806. Although he returned to London with a non-examined, non-residential degree, the Royal College of Physicians was accepting candidates with Aberdeen and even St Andrews degrees provided they had proof that they had attended a university for two years, and the overwhelming majority had, like Knighton, attended Edinburgh. He presented himself for examination as a Licentiate in early May, and during the next two months undertook three oral examinations in Latin, each lasting an hour or so. He finally became a Licentiate on 25 June, free to practise as a physician. However he had yet to establish himself in London, and in late August or early September Dorothea became pregnant.

1797–1809: The Young Doctor

The *Memoirs* described Knighton's progress on his return to London in 1806 as certain and sustained, and include a letter in which he described it as surpassing his expectations. Nevertheless people whom Dorothea termed his 'relations and connexions' in Devon urged him to return to Plymouth, and an anecdote from James Northcote suggests that Knighton's progress was far from certain. Speaking when Knighton was at the height of his influence, Northcote revelled in a yarn about the struggling young doctor. According to Northcote, when Knighton returned to London from Edinburgh he spent many an unemployed hour visiting the Northcotes and despairing at the slowness of his practice. Northcote told Knighton that that was the experience of every man in every profession at the beginning of a London career and that he must stick it out and live on potatoes if necessary.

According to Northcote, the Knightons hoped that Dorothea's skill at landscapes would assist in 'making the pot boil', but he doubted whether it answered much. Dorothea's talent was not in question. She was an accomplished copyist, and at auction one of her copies reached twice the price of original works of her professionally-trained son. An exquisite illustration of a feather, preserved in a scrapbook at Plymouth and West Devon Record Office, shows that she was amply qualified to undertake botanical illustration which was respectable paid employment for gentlewomen. It was, however, a woman from a less respectable but more lucrative profession who came to Knighton's aid. Northcote recalled that one day Knighton positively swaggered into the Northcotes' home and scandalised them by swinging a leg over the arm of a chair as he sat down. From now on, he announced, they would be seeing a lot less of him. Harangued for his conduct, he calmed down and told them that he was suddenly receiving recommendation after recommendation. The key to his changed fortunes was, he explained, a certain new patient.

Chapter 3
1809–1817: Into Society

The patient who opened London society to Knighton was a courtesan named Sally Douglas, also known as Poll or Moll Raffles, or Mrs Lashley. Her more famous professional contemporary, Harriette Wilson, called her a rich woman, but it was Douglas's connections, rather than the money at her command, that mattered to Knighton. Writing to his brother-in-law, Seymour, to explain his decision to remain in London, he described his progress as being constantly handed over by one circle of people to another. Such was the 'immensity' of London that if the original contacts were lost they were not missed and the new ones might prove more valuable. Douglas was just such a link. Her current benefactor was a former Member of Parliament for Bere Alston – Richard Wellesley, Marquess Wellesley, a man who appreciated ability, inspired loyalty, and rewarded both.

Richard Wellesley was the eldest of five Irish Protestant brothers. On his father's death in 1781 he inherited the titles of Viscount Wellesley and Earl of Mornington and gave up his studies at Oxford to become head of the family and settle his brothers in careers. His middle brother, Arthur, became Duke of Wellington in 1814 because of his military victories but, in an age when army commissions had to be bought, it was Richard who had rescued Arthur's career more than twenty years earlier by giving him the money to become a major. For eight years until 1805 Richard Wellesley was Governor-General of India and he was made marquess for his services there. India was then vital for British trade but not for Britain's physical security, and was administered by the East India Company, not by the British Government. During Richard Wellesley's governorship Britain had done much to consolidate its physical and administrative control of India. Britain, however, under threat of invasion from Napoleon, was not interested in the future jewel in the crown. Ahead of his time in India, Richard Wellesley was out of step with events at home, for in October

1805, when Nelson staved off the immediate threat of invasion by defeating the French at Trafalgar at the cost of his own life, Richard Wellesley was sailing back from India with reputed savings of £100,000 and a retinue whose wine bill threatened to bankrupt the ship's captain.

Moreover Richard's absence in India broke his marriage. Anchored off Spithead on 7 January 1806, he wrote a brief though loving note to his wife, Hyacinthe, but after their reunion at Portsmouth days later he fell violently and irrevocably out of love with the loyal, intelligent but not uncritical woman whom he married after the birth of their fifth child and whose brief career as a Parisian actress made her unacceptable to his family. Historian Iris Butler recognised the importance of Hyacinthe's letters and translated them from the French originals for her biography of Richard Wellesley. Hyacinthe's chronicle of the end of her marriage, and Butler's analysis of Richard Wellesley's career, explain much about Knighton's life between 1807 and 1812.

Hyacinthe believed that her husband's relationship with Douglas started in April 1807. Fearful for her children, who because of their parents' late marriage would not inherit the Wellesley titles, Hyacinthe berated Wellesley for keeping 'la Douglas', as she called her, in inappropriate luxury, making a fool of himself and damaging the prospects of his entire family. Knighton appeared in Hyacinthe's letters as 'the accoucheur' – that is, an obstetrician or man-midwife – or 'a certain doctor'. She believed that he was treating her husband for unnamed lifestyle diseases and that he was part of a retinue of sycophants separating father from family.

By then Knighton was sufficiently well known to return a favour and support an application for a medical degree from King's College, Aberdeen from the partner of Ralph Blegborough, the London accoucheur who had vouched for Knighton at Aberdeen only a year earlier. After returning to London Knighton had taken a huge risk. Between spring 1806 and spring 1807, the very time when Northcote was advising him to live on potatoes, Knighton took a lease on 9 Hanover Square, the London address by which he became known. Argyll Street had been respectable and professional.

Hanover Square, only a few hundred yards west, was fashionable. No 9 was long and narrow and twenty years older than No 28, but its previous occupant had been Dr Robert Hallifax, a physician to George, Prince of Wales. The gamble succeeded. In October 1807 Knighton was one of fourteen accoucheurs who met to petition the Royal Colleges of Physicians and Surgeons to have their specialty regulated. They included Blegborough, who was becoming an acknowledged expert, and septuagenarian Thomas Denman, who had been a leading London accoucheur in the 1780s but who now only undertook consultations. Also present were Denman's son-in-law, Richard Croft, who had taken over his practice, and John Sims who, with Croft, would attend the ill-fated confinement of George's daughter, Princess Charlotte, in 1817. More than half the petitioners were older than Knighton, some by more than forty years, and most held hospital appointments or wrote medical articles. The farmer's son was in eminent professional company.

Between 1808 and 1809 Knighton attended Richard Wellesley at the resort of Ramsgate where, according to Hyacinthe, the Archbishop of Canterbury's family observed Wellesley in the servant's seat of a carriage used by ladies of the street. Richard Wellesley was suffering personal and professional crises, for in addition to his broken marriage he was without employment. Richard Wellesley was acceptable to both political parties of the day, the Whigs and the Tories. His political mentor had been the younger William Pitt, the charismatic Tory Prime Minister, and he was a close friend of a leading Whig family, the Grenvilles. However for three years Wellesley refused public office while he refuted allegations of fraud connected with his governorship of India. Finally, in the spring of 1809 Richard Wellesley accepted from the coalition Government of William Bentinck, Duke of Portland, the post of Special Ambassador to the Spanish Central Junta, and asked Knighton to accompany him. The post was temporary and Seymour noted that Knighton would return to his practice in a few months when the mission was over. Wellesley's immediate superior was the Foreign Secretary, George Canning, who had also been mentored by the younger

Pitt. Canning found it difficult to work with the Secretary of State for War, Robert Stewart, Viscount Castlereagh, whom he wished to replace with Richard Wellesley. While Richard was in Spain Stewart's uncle, who was also a member of the Government, would explain to Stewart that he should resign.

Knighton and Dorothea now had a child, Dora, and at the end of May a Dr Knighton, Mrs Knighton and Miss Knighton sat for George Engleheart, miniature painter to George III; these were perhaps the pictures of his wife and daughter that Knighton took to Spain and the picture of himself that he hoped would help prevent little Dora from forgetting him. He left London on 22 July and was soon homesick, declaring only three weeks later, 'I have felt this separation so much, that nothing shall tempt me to consent to it a second time.' In his letters home he told Dorothea that he had gone to Spain to make her and Dora 'a little more independent' and hasten their 'virtuous retirement' to 'some peaceful and happy cottage' with a little land. In practice the Peninsula visit enabled Knighton to prove that his abilities were not limited to medicine.

For the first part of the journey from London to Portsmouth Knighton travelled with Benjamin Sydenham, Richard Wellesley's confidential aide. As Knighton told Dorothea, Sydenham 'possessed most justly Lord Wellesley's entire confidence'. In return 'his affection was completely with his lordship'. Finding himself alone with Knighton, Sydenham sounded out the new man. There were unmistakable parallels between their lives – Sydenham too had lacked money and connections, and he too was ambitious, intelligent and dedicated to self-improvement. Knighton enjoyed Sydenham's company but stopped short of identifying with him, perhaps because Sydenham was keeping house with one of Harriette Wilson's sisters. Sydenham recounted an anecdote that combined life after death, always an emotive subject with Knighton, with politics, a not unimportant subject with Wellesley. According to Sydenham, William Pitt the Younger, a Tory, and Charles Fox, a radical Whig, 'had both examined the records of Scripture with scrupulous care, with a view of satisfying their minds as to a future state'. Sydenham told Knighton that he had been unable to ascertain Mr Fox's views. Would Knighton, thrown off balance by a reminder of his son's death, blurt out a detailed and sympathetic appraisal of Fox's beliefs? Knighton was, after all, a friend of James Northcote, who had radical sympathies. Returning to England while the rest of Wellesley's entourage remained in Spain, Sydenham found time to visit Dorothea and Dora and observe the Knighton household. Meanwhile Knighton experienced the benefits of serving Richard Wellesley. Interesting, intelligent people treated him with courtesy and respect, and he was routinely alone with Wellesley, not only as his employee but as a companion, for Richard Wellesley's manner was to include his subordinates in his life.

The Central Junta was a government of resistance which was ruling Spain because Napoleon had forced the Spanish king to abdicate. British policy was to support Portugal and Spain in their resistance to Napoleon, and Richard Wellesley's main tasks were to encourage the Spanish Junta to rule more effectively, and to convince them that, if they wanted British troops to help defeat the French, they would have to feed them. Knighton's official position in Wellesley's staff was that of personal physician, but he wrote to Dorothea of duties that he hoped to fulfil 'speedily and safely'. He had daily meetings at a set time with Richard Wellesley, after which he 'digested' what Wellesley had told him. He suffered 'fatiguing' exercise of his mind, and summed up the trip by saying that he had had 'an arduous, anxious, and delicate situation' and had been entrusted with 'different things'. These comments would be more apt for a trusted aide, and Richard Wellesley was short of one such man. His brother Henry was to have accompanied him as chief secretary to the embassy, but only Iris Butler has noticed that Henry did not in fact take up his new post. In March 1809 Henry's wife eloped, leaving him too ill and distraught to go to Spain. Whether Knighton took over Henry's duties in full or in part, and if so, whether by accident or design, is unknown. However at the end of the trip Knighton praised Richard Wellesley's 'ability and extraordinary talents', concluding that it was impossible to serve under his direction without loving him, while Sydenham described the warmth and affection with which Richard Wellesley had expressed his 'entire approbation' of Knighton.

Richard Wellesley's party embarked for Spain on 24 July and returned to Portsmouth in late November 1809, summoned back as a result of bizarre events at home. Stewart had become suspicious at a Cabinet meeting in early September 1809 and subsequently learnt the truth at dinner. Stewart, Canning and Bentinck, who in any case had recently suffered a stroke, all resigned at various stages. Historians dwell on the subsequent duel between Stewart and Canning, but the true significance of the episode is that in the middle of a war Britain lost its Secretaries of State for War and for the Foreign Office, and its Prime Minister. Richard Wellesley was not implicated in the concealment and cherished not unreasonable hopes of becoming Prime Minister. In the event he accepted an equivalent position to that which Canning had promised him, becoming Foreign Secretary in the Tory Government of Spencer Perceval. As Seymour predicted, Knighton returned to Hanover Square and his practice.

At the height of his success as a physician Knighton earned £10,000 a year, but we have only scant details of how he conducted his practice. One of his few close friends, Benjamin Brodie, a respected surgeon, wrote that Knighton socialised little and so was 'always to be found'. Because gentlemen did not charge each other for kindnesses, top physicians did not ask for fees. Instead they accepted whatever sums their patients 'intended' for them, trusting that the higher the patient's self-worth, the larger the cheque to the physician. It was a risky strategy for Knighton who, unlike many of his colleagues, did not hold a hospital or teaching appointment. The British Library holds a letter from Knighton to Wellesley dated 22 July 1809, the day on which he left London for the Peninsula, respectfully acknowledging a cheque for £3,000. In handwriting that was elegant and easy on the eye, Knighton offered his thanks to Wellesley 'in the strongest manner' but did not say what the money was for. Knighton treated the family of radical publisher Leigh Hunt without charge and occasionally lent him money. Leigh Hunt was however a friend of the aristocratic poet, George Byron, who made regular, modest payments to Knighton but who was a prestigious patient.

An important source of information for this period of Knighton's life is *Regency Memoirs* by Richard Grenville, a Whig and one of Knighton's contemporaries. *Regency Memoirs* included a letter from January 1812 that described Knighton as being at the head of his profession as an accoucheur. It said that where he became intimate with a household he soon became influential, and that as a result he had the 'key-note' of almost every family of distinction in the country – in other words, he understood what motivated them – and that he was especially influential at Lansdowne House, the home of a prominent Whig family. By spring 1815 Robert Gooch was taking the overflow of Knighton's patients, but despite their numbers they are hard to identify. The *Memoirs* named only Byron and Lady Catherine Stepney, a novelist. A footnote in Arthur Aspinall's article on Knighton and George IV has Knighton treating George Canning's young daughter Harriet, born in 1804, but there is no evidence that Knighton treated Canning's son, George, who was a chronic invalid. Harriette Wilson wrote that in the summer of 1815 Knighton attended her sister Fanny, who was dying. Judith Schneid Lewis frequently refers to Knighton in *Childbearing in the British Aristocracy* but, of his patients, names only Charlotte Grimston, Lady Verulam, whose brother, Robert Banks Jenkinson, Lord Liverpool, was Prime Minister during most of Knighton's years at Court.

The research of Judith Schneid Lewis portrays the accoucheur's life as one of limited remedies and long hours of physically and emotionally exhausting work. Despite Knighton's reputation for tact and taste he was no cerebral aesthete. He achieved financial independence by easing the new-born aristocracy from their mothers' birth canals at unsociable hours while contending with blue blood, faeces and urine. As his profession was later cited as justification for blocking his advancement it is worth knowing what it entailed. The following account is based on Judith Schneid Lewis's comprehensive description.

An accoucheur's aim was to make the patient's body regulate itself so that she would conceive, carry her baby for its full term, survive labour and give birth to a healthy child, and this brought him into prolonged contact with the patient and her household. Most pregnant women were considered to be plethoric – that is, to have too much blood – in which case accoucheurs prescribed a 'lowering regimen' of plain food and washing with cool water. Despite the accoucheurs' holistic ideals the lowering regimen also included the removal of blood, known as bleeding, by cutting a vein, scraping the skin or by applying leeches. Most aristocratic British women went to London to give birth, especially if a first son was hoped for, and if necessary the accoucheur arranged his patient's accommodation, leasing a house and hiring medical attendants. One of these was the monthly nurse who arrived a few days before the birth to help with the preparations and who was capable of delivering the baby on her own if necessary. If the accoucheur expected labour to be difficult he might arrange for another physician to be present. In early September 1816 Knighton was accompanied on a consultation by Christopher Pemberton, a royal physician whose appointment pre-dated Knighton's, but we do not know whether they attended a confinement.

Two rooms in the house were appropriated for the birth – one for the mother and her attendants and another nearby for her visitors – and although in Knighton's day many lying-in rooms were still kept darkened, the best were cool and well ventilated. To give birth the mother-to-be wore a shift with its hem rolled back and tucked under her arms and a short petticoat round her waist, and she lay on a special folding bed that positioned her at the best height for her medical attendants. She was placed on her left side – for a gentleman was always right-handed – with her back to the edge of the bed where the accoucheur could reach her genitals to deliver her baby without making eye contact. He was assisted by the monthly nurse, and many accoucheurs always worked with the same nurse. Dorothea took pains to include in the *Memoirs* all those who were important to Knighton, and his nurse was perhaps 'poor Mrs. —' who by 1825 was the Knightons' pensioner.

Knighton and his nurse could give the mother certain routine help. They could help prevent her perineum from splitting by applying lubrication and supporting her buttocks in their hands. They could make sure that she had emptied her bowels and bladder. If labour became prolonged Knighton could catheterise her. Medical opinion at the time held that a long labour was not harmful and that forceps should not be used until six hours after the last contraction. The mother's life always came first, and as a last resort the accoucheur broke the foetus's skull and removed its body piecemeal. Once the placenta had been removed the accoucheur's job was over. Mother's soiled petticoat was removed, her clean shift pulled down and she was moved to the dry, comfortable centre of the bed. The accoucheur told the waiting family how many visitors his patient was strong enough to see, and went home. The nurse took charge of mother and baby for the remainder of the allotted month and administered any medicines that the accoucheur prescribed.

Benjamin Brodie described Knighton as a physician with 'no scientific attainments' but 'much practical knowledge'. By 1812 Knighton was in his mid-thirties and been involved in medicine for nineteen years. He had trained as an apothecary, been a general practitioner, treated battle injuries and ship fevers, mixed with all classes of people and studied under the top lecturers of the age. His progress in medicine is recorded in his own words.

In July 1798, a few months after the death of Francis Geach, Knighton made one of his first independent consultations and wrote a diagnosis. His patient, Thomas Byam Martin, naval officer and later a Plymouth Member of Parliament, kept it as a curiosity when Knighton rose to power. It is now in the British Library, accompanied by Byam's unnecessary observation that he had seen Knighton's mother selling butter and eggs at Plymouth market. In his early twenties Knighton wrote in a scrappy, mannered hand, the tails of his 'ds' curling backwards and an irritating flourish to each lower-case 's'. Desperate to display his self-taught knowledge, obtained against the odds, Knighton littered his diagnosis with classical allusions.

He attempted, but failed, to write as his patient's social equal. However his medical knowledge was sound, the case astutely observed.

Two years later Knighton published his pamphlet on the use of mercury for treating 'putrid fever and putrid sore throats', printing it at his own expense. The Wellcome Library holds a copy, a quality publication with clear black type on sturdy paper. Instead of citing the classics Knighton provided factual examples of symptoms and treatment and he structured his argument. The form of mercury that he recommended was calomel, which treats the tissues with which it comes into contact but which is less poisonous than traditional mercury because it is less easily absorbed into the bloodstream. Knighton contended that although calomel was considered a laxative, its action was limited to evacuating foul substances, so it could even be used to treat dysentery. He explained that he was discussing an observation that had already found favour among senior physicians, and included copy correspondence to support his claim. The theory had already appeared in print and Knighton pre-empted accusations of plagiarism by making it clear that he was citing the empirical findings of other practitioners. Indeed he made a virtue of the fact that calomel had been used many times with success. With Britain at war on land and at sea, Knighton made his work pertinent by describing how William Bredall, charged with the care of 120 soldiers among whom 'putrid fever' was rife, cured all but one with mercury. Knighton then gave examples of its use in fevers contracted at sea. He concluded with a respectful urging of scientific enquiry to justify his cautious digression from established practice.

It is difficult to judge whether the treatment that Knighton proposed was an improvement on established practice or even whether it was viable. Medical terminology has changed and we cannot be sure for what diseases he intended it. 'Putrid fever' was probably typhus and 'putrid and ulcerated sore throat' was probably diphtheria, which is usually but not exclusively a childhood disease. The pamphlet does, however, say a great deal about Knighton's medical beliefs. He followed an 'antiphlogistic' regimen for diseases, of which the 'lowering regimen' was a logical extension. Medical practitioners believed that their patients became ill because of impurities in the blood. Doctors sought to make the body flush itself out through vomiting, sweating, salivation, urination and defecation by prescribing, respectively, emetics, heat, ptyalagogues, diuretics and purgatives such as those prescribed by Astley Cooper for Hall Overend. It was a labour-intensive way of treating a patient requiring constant observation, for which all those years of writing up case notes for Geach were the ideal training. A new medication was required at each stage of the illness; Knighton noted that once the calomel had rid the body of foul stools, Bredall occasionally found it necessary to prescribe a gentle laxative. Medical men also believed that inflammation was caused by excess blood, which they removed by bleeding. Despite the limitations of his profession, Knighton was a commonsense, practical physician. In the Peninsula he stayed free of vermin by sleeping in his own portable bed and he avoided the local water.

A friend wrote that Knighton was remarkable for the ascendancy that he exercised over his patients' minds, much for their benefit – in other words, he persuaded them back to health – and it was because of Knighton's powers of persuasion that Richard Wellesley considered him qualified to serve the highest family in the land. In November 1811 George, then Prince of Wales, became unwell while staying at Oatlands, the home of his eldest brother, Frederick, Duke of York. George was acting as regent for his father, George III, who was suffering his final and most debilitating attack of porphyria. At that time George had only limited powers, but in another three months the limitations would end and he would become the Prince Regent, King in all but name and the deciding influence over who formed his Governments. Richard Wellesley was a frequent visitor to Oatlands and endeared himself to George by being good company and by saying that any Government should pay George's debts and increase his Civil List allowance. Richard Wellesley recommended George to consult Knighton, who attended at once. Professional etiquette prevented Knighton from recommending any treatment as George was already under the care of three senior physicians, but the consultation was only a ruse.

1809–1817: Into Society

As Richard Wellesley hoped, Knighton made a sufficiently good impression for George to conclude that this well-mannered, well-connected doctor was someone he would like for himself, and in January 1812 Knighton became one of George's physicians-in-ordinary, taking the vacancy created by the death of Robert Hallifax in September 1810. But whereas Hallifax had initially received the lesser post of physician-extraordinary, Knighton was immediately given the more senior post. It gave him access to George's household where, Whig contemporaries believed, Wellesley had deliberately placed him. *Regency Memoirs* included a letter describing Knighton's 'extreme' devotion to Richard Wellesley. To those Whigs who thought that Richard Wellesley would side with them, Knighton's appointment was looked on 'as a great achievement, and likely to keep all matters steady in future'. Wellesley's complicity is beyond doubt. On 3 January 1812 he wrote to George's private secretary, John McMahon. Following an audience with the Prince Regent he was, he said, 'led to hope' that Knighton's appointment would be announced in the *London Gazette* the following day and, after some belt-and-braces praise of Knighton, Wellesley reminded McMahon of the *Gazette*'s two-o'clock deadline.

A year later, in January 1813, Knighton was made, or 'created', a baronet. A baronetcy is the sixth of seven degrees of rank that can be conferred by the monarch. Below Knighton were knights whose titles died with them; above him were peers – barons, viscounts, earls, marquesses and, top of the list, dukes – whose titles were inherited by their eldest sons. In Knighton's day peers automatically sat in the House of Lords, the second chamber of Parliament, to support or oppose the Government. Baronets could not sit in the Lords but they could pass their titles to their eldest sons. Accepting a baronetcy meant paying a 400 guinea patent fee, but the benefits lasted for generations. The historical novelist Walter Scott, who became a baronet in 1820, told Knighton that the certainty of inheriting a title enabled his eldest son to be accepted by a young lady of fortune and marry during Scott's lifetime; only after Scott's death could he have afforded marriage to a less wealthy woman. Royal physicians were frequently but not automatically awarded baronetcies – Robert Hallifax was not so honoured despite twenty-five years' service in the royal household. For Knighton to receive a baronetcy only a year after his appointment, having never treated George and having made no contribution to medical science, was exceptional. Knighton was not preoccupied by his title. For his arms and crest he adapted those granted to an unrelated Knighton in Hertfordshire in 1634. However a baronetcy would increase his prestige and his practice, and he now had a son to inherit the title – William Wellesley Knighton, born in January 1811.

Those who accepted their sovereign's mark of distinction tacitly agreed to live according to their rank, and by the spring of 1814 Knighton had acquired a home fit for a baronet. Robert Gooch once wrote to Knighton saying that he had had a long refreshing sleep for the first time in weeks, adding, 'I dreamt I was at Sherwood with you and Lady Knighton'. This was not an allusion to Robin Hood but Sherwood Lodge on the Wandsworth–Battersea border. A sales catalogue at Woking Family Records Centre describes it at the time Knighton sold it in 1820. Sherwood Lodge was not the cottage for which the homesick Knighton had longed five years earlier but a villa on the banks of the Thames at Battersea set in six acres of pleasure grounds. It was modern, comfortable and convenient. The produce of its kitchen garden, vinery, peachery, strawberry house, mushroom sheds, dairy, cow shed, piggery and poultry yard were prepared in a kitchen whose scullery had water laid on, and eaten either in the 'Eating Room', whose bordered walls were decorated with coloured compartments and whose pillars were finished in imitation verd-antique, or in the banqueting or 'Tent Room' which had sliding doors of stained glass. Afterwards the ladies retired to the 'elegant bowed drawing room' with Parisian-fringed chintz draperies and a clouded ceiling; the men to the dome-lit, basso-relievoed billiard room. There were water-closets in every bedroom and a 'capital bath room', with bath, lined with Dutch tiles. To lift the spirits in fine weather were 'Lawns, fine gravelled Walks, Parterres, Planted with luxuriant Shrubs, Flowers, Evergreens, and stately Timber Trees' and a

Hermitage 'neatly enclosed by Trellis Work'. Indoors was a one-hundred-and-eight-foot marble-paved conservatory-cum-orangery with an aviary for birds and a pond for gold and silver fish. A dome-lit octagonal library and a seventy-five foot statuary gallery catered for the intellect. Colour and decoration dazzled the eyes and senses, and the whole was light and airy. Exit was via landing steps from 'a delightful Terrace Walk along the banks of the River'.

The vendor was Jens Wolff, the son of a naturalised Dane and a partner in Wolff & D'Orville, successful importers of Norwegian timber. Wolff was a generous and imaginative host under whom Sherwood Lodge was a salon. The artist Joseph Farington described arriving by water one July evening with Thomas Lawrence, later one of George's favourite painters and president of the Royal Academy, to dine under a tent of many colours upon a carpet spread on the lawn in front of the Thames. On another occasion the statue gallery was lit by candles when darkness fell. In June 1811 Wolff gave a grand public breakfast for, so the reports said, four or five hundred 'personages of distinction'. Soon afterwards, however, Wolff & D'Orville became bankrupt. They had lost a reputed £455,000 worth of vessels during the war but been unable to obtain compensation. Wolff sold Sherwood Lodge and the Knightons moved into their surprising choice of home.

The Knightons' last child, Mary Frances, named after Knighton's Tavistock aunts, and William Wellesley, whose middle name acknowledged Knighton's patron, were christened at their parish church of St Mary's, Battersea. Richard Wellesley stood godfather to the child named for him. Giving a child someone else's surname as a middle name was not only a tribute but an insurance should the child need to claim its namesake's help. Standing godfather recognised the claim. With Knighton and Wellesley however it was recognition of a debt. Wellesley's career had peaked. He would never again hold a Cabinet post, for sharing common ground with both Whigs and Tories left him in complete agreement with neither. On 16 January 1812, only a fortnight after placing Knighton in

George's household, Richard Wellesley had resigned as Foreign Secretary on a matter of conscience. Neither George nor the Tory Government to which Wellesley belonged would support Catholic emancipation – that is, removing the remaining restrictions on Roman Catholics which prevented them from becoming Members of Parliament. Richard could not support the Whigs either, because they wanted to end the war with Napoleonic France. In the summer of 1812 gunshot again raised Richard Wellesley's hopes. Perceval was assassinated and George asked Richard Wellesley to form a coalition Government. Wellesley, however, could not find enough people to serve under him. Worse, in the process he deeply offended the eventual Prime Minister, Robert Banks Jenkinson, who remained in power until 1827.

When Richard Wellesley resigned as Foreign Secretary, his son felt obliged to resign his own Government post at the Treasury. Knighton was under no such obligation. His debt to Richard Wellesley was not in conflict with his position at Court for the post of physician-in-ordinary was in George's gift, independent of the Government of the day. Knighton could in all conscience use the ability that Wellesley had recognised in him to benefit from the post in which Wellesley had placed him. Like Sally Douglas, Richard Wellesley had handed Knighton on to another circle of people. The new circle included John McMahon, George's private secretary. By the summer of 1817 McMahon was terminally ill and he resigned his post, possibly at Knighton's suggestion. Dosing himself with alcohol, the substance that had caused his decline, McMahon was becoming indiscreet. He had it in his power to cast doubt on George's fitness to be King and possibly to exclude him from the throne. What could be more natural than for George to send one of his own physicians – but not a senior man, who would attract attention – to enquire after McMahon's health?

Chapter 4
1817–1822: Into Royal Favour

After his visit to the dying McMahon Knighton appeared more and more frequently in George's presence, and his sudden rise in royal favour after five undistinguished years as physician-in-ordinary mystified his contemporaries. Many assumed that Knighton had achieved his success through dishonourable means, and not until the publication of Aspinall's *Letters* more than a hundred years after the deaths of both George and Knighton did the events of 1817 become clear. Knighton emerges as neither schemer nor saint but as a man who, presented by fate with an opportunity that would never be repeated, saw nothing dishonourable in making his talents known.

McMahon was the son of a butler who had married a fellow servant, and in the context of a royal household he was a likely ally for a farmer's son. When McMahon made his will in 1816 he left Knighton £500 in token of 'kind Services', but the relationship was not as close as contemporaries assumed. Although Knighton occasionally treated McMahon, McMahon named another physician as the 'Long preserver' of his life, and a half-brother, Sir William McMahon, as his executor. The man to whom McMahon was closest was his secretary, Thomas Marrable, the son of a provincial bookseller. By 1816 Marrable was nearly thirty and had been in the royal household for the past ten years. Describing Marrable as his 'Excellent & kind ffriend [sic]', McMahon left him £2,000. More importantly McMahon used his will to recommend Marrable to George, specifically bequeathing Marrable as 'an invaluable Servant' to 'the Best Hearted Man on Earth the Prince Regent'.

Knighton detested McMahon's wife and believed that she took bribes from place-seekers. However he described McMahon as a complete courtier yet good-hearted, honest and a sincere friend. Like Knighton, McMahon had had a poor education, but whereas Knighton had trained in a profession that would earn him ready money, McMahon had chosen, or had had chosen for him, the uncertainties of army life. In 1775, aged about twenty-one, he went to America to fight in the War of Independence and attracted the patronage of Francis Rawdon, later Francis Rawdon Hastings and Earl of Moira. Hastings was an aristocratic officer who in the 1790s became one of George's political allies. As Prince of Wales with as yet no regency powers, George colluded with the Whigs in opposition to his Tory father, George III. Through Hastings' influence McMahon entered George's household in 1800, in the same way that Richard Wellesley placed Knighton in George's household in 1812. McMahon's appointment, however, was overtly political, for in 1802 Hastings and another Whig officer arranged for McMahon to become a Member of Parliament. The practice of the age was to reward unpaid service with a sinecure – a salaried job that involved only token duties, or no duties at all – and McMahon held at least one post whose title did not perhaps reflect his work for George.

In 1812, when George became full Regent, McMahon's duties became more precisely defined. McMahon held three working posts under George – private secretary, Keeper of the Privy Purse and auditor of the Duchy of Cornwall – and he resigned his seat in Parliament. The posts of Privy Purse and auditor were complementary. The Duchy of Cornwall is a portfolio of property and investments created in the fourteenth century to provide an income for the monarch's eldest son, the Prince of Wales, and as Keeper of the Privy Purse McMahon dealt with George's private income and expenditure. In addition McMahon became a Privy Councillor, which meant that he was on equal footing with senior members of the Government in being required to advise the monarch. Unfortunately on the death of his wife in 1815 he took to drink. By the summer of 1817 the trusted McMahon, privy to nearly two decades of royal secrets, was fast losing his mind. By mid-July he had been persuaded to resign on grounds of ill health, though he was sufficiently clear headed to make it known that his resignation made him eligible to return to Parliament.

Knighton's actions regarding George's papers and the dying McMahon were the most controversial of his career at Court. He himself left two

1817–1822: Into Royal Favour

versions of events. One, written in 1830, is in both Aspinall's *Letters* and, heavily amended, in the *Memoirs*. More reliable is a letter that appears as a footnote in the *Letters* and which Knighton wrote to George on 18 August 1817 without the benefit of hindsight. Knighton reported that on Saturday, 16 August 1817 he had, in obedience to George's command, visited McMahon's home at Blackheath only to find that McMahon had left for town. Knighton waited. When McMahon returned Knighton found him mentally and physically enfeebled as a result of having been heavily bled. Knighton administered brandy and water and McMahon's sanity returned.

On Sunday, 17 August Knighton went to Blackheath again, contriving that Marrable should also be present. It is clear from the letter of 18 August that Knighton was not, as his contemporaries believed, acting on his own initiative. He was following a plan that was perhaps of his own devising but which he had agreed beforehand with George. The first part of the plan was to ascertain McMahon's state of mind and to retrieve from him certain papers. This was managed in such a way that McMahon, who was still lucid, instructed Marrable to place himself under Knighton's instructions and to hand over whatever Knighton asked for. The second part of the plan revealed that George now trusted Knighton completely. Knighton reported that in accordance with George's instructions he had taken all the papers home to Hanover Square and locked them in his own safe. He was now, he told George, reading every scrap of paper and cataloguing those that he believed George should keep. Marrable had acted 'with great propriety of conduct' at Blackheath, and unless George ordered otherwise 'no second person' – Knighton being the first person – would read the papers retrieved from McMahon. Another royal prince might have considered Knighton's actions unpardonable presumption, but Knighton had the measure of his master. George was happy to avoid both the tedium of reading the documents and any disconcerting memories they held.

Presumably to avoid painful reminders and lest his letter should fall into hostile hands, Knighton did not specify what the documents were. In the letter of 18 August he described them as 'all your Royal Highness's private letters, early correspondence and other documents' and as 'your [George's] early correspondence or early documents of any description'. The papers may have been merely embarrassing or they may have related to an event that compromised George's right to become King. In a clandestine ceremony in December 1785 George, then Prince of Wales, had married Maria Fitzherbert, a Roman Catholic widow. As Flora Fraser, the biographer of George's second wife, Caroline, explains, the Fitzherbert marriage had constitutional implications. Under the Bill of Rights 1689 and the Act of Settlement 1700, if George married a Roman Catholic he could not become King, and according to the canon law of both the Church of England and the Roman Catholic Church his marriage to Fitzherbert was valid. However under the Royal Marriages Act 1772, which took precedence over canon law, the marriage was invalid because George had entered into it without first obtaining the consent of his father, George III. Fitzherbert considered the ceremony binding even though she and George later parted and, whatever the legal position, George had acted in bad faith and shown poor judgment. A decade later he further compromised himself. By then he had run up huge debts, and to appease Parliament into clearing them he had, despite the ceremony with Fitzherbert, done his duty as heir to the throne and married a suitable woman. His bride was Princess Caroline of Brunswick, whom he had detested on sight and from whom he soon separated but by whom he had a daughter, Princess Charlotte.

Although Knighton was devoting a great amount of time to the offending documents he remained in private practice. McMahon's successor was not Marrable but Benjamin Bloomfield, a former Hussars officer. Bloomfield was at first one of George's social acquaintances, not entering George's household until 1812. Like McMahon, Bloomfield held various appointments that may or may not have been connected with the services he performed for George, and Bloomfield too was a Member of Parliament until he became private secretary, though for the Tories, for as acting monarch George no longer supported the Whigs. Importantly, Bloomfield also became a Privy Councillor. Though he had been George's companion for many years his promotion was not a success. In January 1818 Knighton replaced him as auditor of the Duchy of Cornwall. Only a few months into his new post, Bloomfield was being edged out by the new royal favourite. Having done no wrong he received an annuity in lieu. To minimise any awkwardness for George, Knighton arranged the annuity.

As a physician Knighton had a greater than usual experience of comforting the bereaved, and during the next three years George suffered repeated losses. In November 1817 his only legitimate child, Princess Charlotte, died after giving birth to a stillborn male child, and two heirs to the throne were lost in one night. A year later George's mother, Queen Charlotte, died. His father, George III, died on 29 January 1820, and a brother, the Duke of Kent, soon after. George's reaction to each bereavement was to become ill, and when George was ill in early February 1820 Knighton was one of three doctors to sign medical bulletins. His place at Court was now established. On the evening of 16 February 1820 Knighton walked in the procession at Windsor Castle that accompanied the old King to his funeral in St George's Chapel. The old reign ended and Knighton, now in his early forties, emerged from St George's Chapel as physician to the new King of England.

In private Knighton was also George's confidant. For the past two years George had been preparing to get rid of his official wife, Caroline. Previously George had desisted from divorcing or disowning Caroline for fear of jeopardising Princess Charlotte's right to the throne. Charlotte's death removed that obstacle. George had two options. First, he could divorce Caroline, with the risk that Caroline would raise counter allegations, possibly relating to the 1785 marriage. Even if the Fitzherbert marriage were deemed illegal it would show George in such a poor light that the nation might not accept him as King. Secondly, George could prove that Caroline was not fit to be Queen. Knighton looked to his contacts.

Since 1814 Caroline had led a peripatetic bohemian life in Europe and she was now living in Italy. One of Knighton's fellow students at Edinburgh had been Henry Southey, whose brother, Robert, was poet laureate. In the summer of 1817 Robert Southey was in Europe, and in December 1817 Knighton reported to George that he had obtained from Robert Southey a 'paper' on Caroline's conduct abroad. Knighton's involvement was a logical progression from retrieving documents from McMahon. Aspinall's *Letters* show Knighton assembling evidence, watching the press and pre-empting opposition. The following summer the information-gathering against Caroline was put on a formal footing called the Milan Commission. Knighton was not part of it, perhaps at his own wish, for it was a sordid business involving detailed interviews with her servants abroad.

On the death of his father in January 1820 George became King, and if no action were taken against Caroline she would be entitled to attend his coronation and be crowned Queen. Senior members of the Government advised George on the legal and constitutional implications, but when he became upset and overwrought he turned to Knighton. In April 1820 he sent for Knighton to meet him in London, ending the letter 'God bless you'. At the end of May, when Caroline was known to be travelling across Europe on her way to England, George wrote at night to implore Knighton, now his 'dear friend', to visit the following morning; George could not consider leaving Carlton House until he had seen him. Knighton began to adapt his professional and private lives to accommodate his new role. Robert Gooch took on even more of his patients and, as London became obsessed with unsavoury gossip about Caroline, Knighton bought a small home at Blendworth in Hampshire and sold Sherwood Lodge. The purchaser was, of all people, Maria Fitzherbert.

George's difficulties are explained by Flora Fraser. By the summer of 1820 the Milan Commission had established that while abroad Caroline had failed to behave with the decorum expected of a Queen of England. However George's double standards had by now rendered him an object of ridicule, and Caroline's cause had become entwined with that of political radicalism. George wanted Caroline to be prosecuted, but a trial in court would enable her to make damaging counter-accusations. The head of the English legal system, John Scott, the Lord Chancellor, known as Lord

Eldon, decided instead to deal with Caroline by means of a Bill of Pains and Penalties, a piece of legislation that had to pass through both Houses of Parliament. If successful this particular Bill of Pains and Penalties would strip Caroline of her title and privileges as Queen. Expecting legal action against her, Caroline had already appointed as her legal adviser the reformist lawyer and Member of Parliament, Henry Brougham.

The Bill started in the Lords in August 1820, but in November it passed with such a slim majority that it was abandoned without reaching the Commons – Knighton was present for at least one of the final debates, when he gave medical aid to a former Lord Chancellor who was taken ill while speaking against the Bill and who recovered sufficiently to return and continue his attack. Despite the Bill's defeat Caroline was physically excluded from George's coronation on 19 July 1821, and the sheer spectacle of the celebrations diverted public attention away from a portly foreign princess with dubious morals. Caroline died, conveniently and unexpectedly, in early August.

Too private to find a place in the *Letters,* the *Memoirs* or in any obituary was Dorothy's death on Christmas Eve 1820. In all other respects, Knighton had much to be pleased with. After the coronation George made what would prove to be his only royal tours, visiting Ireland in August 1821, Hanover a month later and Scotland in August 1822. Accompanying him to Hanover and Scotland would be Knighton.

The chain of events that took George to Hanover was more than two centuries old. In 1603 James I had been crowned the first Stuart monarch of Great Britain but, through a combination of unpopularity and obstetric tragedies, his direct descendants failed to continue the dynasty. However in 1658 James's granddaughter Sophia had married the ruler of Hanover, a German state. As a result the kings of Hanover, by then James I's nearest non-Stuart descendants, also became Kings of Britain, starting with George I in 1714 and continuing after George IV's death with his brother William IV – the next British monarch after William IV was Queen Victoria, and the Hanoverian constitution did not allow ruling queens. Each throne had advantages and disadvantages. The British crown was more prestigious and gave indirect access to more money and influence, but to remain Kings of Britain these dual-crown monarchs were required to live in Britain with their powers limited by Parliament. In Hanover however they were barely accountable to the government and could rule from afar. Knighton was confidant to a man who was a constitutional monarch in one country and an absolute monarch in another.

While Bloomfield travelled ahead of the royal suite, Knighton got his first experience of living with George. Gone was the routine of Richard Wellesley's retinue with its morning audience and day's work followed by an early dinner, conversation and music. Knighton slept in an adjoining room so that George, who had no concept of separating day from night or of designating specific times of the day for work and rest, could call on him at all hours. Knighton described himself as 'almost worked to death' with his pen never out of his hand. He did not specify what his duties were, other than putting everything in motion for the departure of the King's suite from Calais to Hanover over roads so bad that the horses had to be changed every five miles.

On becoming king of Hanover George had found it necessary to abolish judicial torture, but even so Knighton liked the place. It was, he wrote home, 'very delightful' and 'much underrated by the English'. He admired the devout, respectful peasants who lined the roads, the arches of greenery erected to honour George and the city streets strewn with flowers and evergreens. At the Palace of Osnabruck he was moved almost to tears when eight thousand people entered the courtyard to sing by torchlight. At night he slept in rooms from the pages of gothic romances and in the morning he looked out over gardens from the pages of fairy tales. Again and again Knighton remarked on his transformation, writing to Dorothea of his Court dress,

> I believe you would hardly know me in my new costume; the whole of it is so comical, that I can scarcely believe my own history. It is more like a romance than anything else.

1817–1822: Into Royal Favour

At Dusseldorf Knighton was bemused by the presence of two hefty Prussian grenadiers outside his bedroom door, and after receiving a Hanoverian honour from George he remarked again to Dorothea how comical it all was, and regretted that his mother was not still alive. This comment was the nearest Knighton got to admitting that Dorothy was an independent, good-humoured Devon farmer whose will had named him as plain 'William Knighton'. His overriding memory of his mother would remain that of the destitute young widow and it would always tug at his heartstrings. During the visit he happened to look out of a window onto a crowded courtyard and see George's Hanoverian chamberlain reject a petition from a woman on bended knees. The despair in her face prompted Knighton to rush downstairs, pushing his way through the crowd for fear of losing sight of her. He discovered that she was the mother of eight young children and that her husband had been sentenced to five years' hard labour for a minor offence. Knighton took her petition to George who immediately granted a pardon. Family ties were not far from Knighton's thoughts. He missed Dorothea and his 'darling dears' – Dora, William and Mary, now aged thirteen, ten and four – and the 'dear cottage at Blendworth'.

When George returned to England his relationship with Bloomfield continued to deteriorate, and it was known that he wished to replace him with Knighton. This involved negotiations between the Government, George and Bloomfield but not with Knighton, who was merely a facilitator. Unlike McMahon and Bloomfield, Knighton was not dependent on George's favour for his livelihood. He had nothing at stake other than the earnings that he lost as a result of unpaid work for George, which he seems to have regarded as an investment, and his auditorship, whose remuneration he could easily recoup in private practice.

Whereas Knighton knew that his profession would always earn him money, Bloomfield had had three years in which to become alarmed and hurt since the loss of his auditorship in 1818. Now in his early fifties he had been out of army life for many years, and of the three parties he had most to lose. The Government regarded the rift between Bloomfield and George as an opportunity to abolish what was considered to be an unconstitutional post. George III had had a private secretary because of his infirmities but under George the post had, in the opinion of both Whigs and Tories, become too influential. Their objections are important as they were later used against Knighton. Because the private secretary liaised between the King and Government ministers he had to be made a Privy Councillor and sworn to secrecy. However as Privy Councillors were duty-bound to advise the monarch, admitting the King's private secretary to the Privy Council turned a clerical post into one with constitutional power. There were also objections on grounds of cost. When George became Regent with limited powers in 1811 he had tried to appoint McMahon as his private secretary but Whig Members of Parliament had challenged the additional charge to the nation. Had McMahon not done the job for a year without pay George would have had to pay him out of his own funds.

George at first tried to get rid of Bloomfield by exploiting the constitutional and financial objections to the post of private secretary. Aspinall's *Letters* contain a letter drafted by Jenkinson, to be sent by George to Bloomfield, which summarised the tactic. George was to tell Bloomfield that he wished the post of the monarch's private secretary to revert to its previous, more clerical status, in which case it would carry a smaller salary. This would severely inconvenience Bloomfield who would instead be found a well-paid post abroad where he would, by implication, be unable to perform his duties as Keeper of the Privy Purse. The letter was drafted in January 1822 but nothing like it was conveyed to Bloomfield until March. By then conveniently damning rumours about Bloomfield's temper, demeanour and honesty had begun to circulate although, like all the most intriguing tales of the period, they were anecdotal.

Believing that his greatest sin had been 'to have loved his Sovereign better than his God', Bloomfield acquiesced to George's wish that he leave the royal household. However he held out for an appointment in a warm foreign court, not too far from England and suitably remunerated. He was finally forced to accept a post in Sweden plus his original auditor's pension, a house at Hampton Court and a sinecure relinquished by its holder as a courtesy to George. Knighton's role was that of calming influence. In a letter of February 1822 he told George that he was confident that nothing unpleasant would happen. George was not to make himself unhappy with apprehension but instead should look after his health, driving for an hour or so each day in an open carriage when the weather permitted. George should mention his intention to do so at dinner, explaining that he was resolved to follow Knighton's recommendation. Knighton ended by saying that he felt untold 'anxiety and misery' on George's behalf. The letter was outrageously unctuous and familiar, and exactly what George wanted to read. Knighton also intervened to ease Bloomfield's feelings. Writing to George in early March after being informed of his imminent dismissal, Bloomfield referred to 'a soothing conversation' that he had just had with Knighton. Bloomfield left Court in early spring. He was to remain Keeper of the Privy Purse so that he could receive its salary until settled in a new post but his Privy Purse duties were temporarily transferred to an official from the Duchy of Cornwall.

The anomalies of the private secretary's post were never resolved and created difficulties for Knighton throughout his years at Court. At the beginning of March 1822 Jenkinson advised George not to introduce Knighton into his household, even as a physician, until Bloomfield had been provided for. George should do nothing more than abolish the post of private secretary. It emerged that the Government did not want George to have a less powerful private secretary. They wanted him to have no private secretary at all. On 23 March 1822 George wrote to Jenkinson pointing out that his original intention had been only to strip the post of the unnecessary power that it had acquired under McMahon and Bloomfield. Nevertheless in the same letter George agreed to try to manage without a private secretary despite the personal inconvenience to himself.

George's acquiescence was disingenuous, for if the Government believed that abolishing the post would stop George having a private secretary they were mistaken. It does indeed seem unreasonable for a monarch to function without a secretary, so to spare George a confrontation with his ministers or further expenditure from the Privy Purse Knighton did the job unofficially and unpaid. He also made it clear to George that he would be no ordinary royal servant. In a letter to George of 10 June 1822 Knighton described himself as 'surrounded with cares' on George's account. They were, Knighton explained, the reason why he had not complied with George's wish that he attend the Royal Lodge at Windsor. He hoped that George would understand that if he, Knighton, was on occasion a lone voice of opposition to George's schemes, it was because he had George's interests at heart. In other words, Knighton's devotion to George's interests was complete; his faith in George's judgment was not. George had probably never received such a letter in his life, and only a financially independent man could have risked writing it.

In August 1822 Knighton sailed with George from Greenwich to Leith. Although the journey was described as a visit to Scotland, George did not stir from Edinburgh. Though once again Knighton's room was near George's, the headaches and hard work of Hanover were not repeated and he found time to search unsuccessfully for his former landlady. More important were two people with whom Knighton had close contact during the Edinburgh visit. One was Edinburgh's famous son, Walter Scott, trained in the law but best known for his historical novels. Despite his popularity as an author Scott was perennially worried about money, and his requests for Knighton's intercession to obtain advancement for his son and assorted favours ended only with George's death. The other was another Edinburgh man, James Wardrop. Wardrop was one of George's surgeons-extraordinary and shared his passion for horses.

All this time Knighton continued in medical practice, and his better-known patients recorded his attendance on them. In April and May of 1820, when George was at his most frantic about Caroline, Knighton attended the three-year-old son of John Wilson Croker, a lawyer best known as an Admiralty official but with an informed interest in literature and art that endeared him to George and won him many friends. The child died. When

1817–1822: Into Royal Favour

George's sister-in-law, the Duchess of Clarence, went into premature labour in December 1820 Knighton was sent for as accoucheur, and he continued in attendance until the baby's death the following March. On 11 July 1821, a week before George's coronation, Knighton responded to a midnight call for help when one of Leigh Hunt's children was dangerously ill. During this time Knighton was also attending Croker's wife, who was still grieving the loss of her son, and on the morning of the coronation Croker went to the Speaker's House at Westminster, where George and his senior officials were dressing for the ceremony, to speak to Knighton about her. In 1822 Knighton attended Charlotte Grimston, the Prime Minister's sister, during her pregnancy. However when George and his suite returned to London in early September that year Knighton drew his practice to a close. He was a reliable, conscientious, skilled and hardworking physician but he was not an outstanding man of medical science. He could progress no further. He was however outstanding at managing George's business. On 10 September 1822, five years after he had administered brandy and water to McMahon, Knighton wrote that the following day would be the last in which he got into his carriage to practise as a physician. The day after that, 12 September, Knighton's appointment as Keeper of the Privy Purse was gazetted. Never again would he write a prescription for money.

The *Memoirs* was ambivalent about Knighton's cessation of his medical practice. Dorothea wrote of 'continued fatigue and anxiety, night and day, and year after year' combined with 'the complete interruption of domestic comfort' suffered by a physician, yet royal service was just as exacting, inconvenient and unpredictable. Although Knighton later claimed that he tolerated George's demands for the sake of his children, he once told George Canning, then Foreign Secretary and later Prime Minister, that by the time he entered George's service he had already made his fortune from his profession. From the gusto with which Knighton entered into all George's concerns during his early years at Court it seems that he simply wanted to do something different. Benjamin Brodie, who knew both Knighton and Dorothea, wrote that Dorothea objected strongly to Knighton joining the royal household. An astute observer, Brodie may well have been right. Nevertheless by 1822, whatever disagreements Dorothea and Knighton may have had about the future, they had already reached a compromise. This had two consequences. The first was Knighton's omission, noted by his contemporaries, to present Dorothea or his children at Court. The second was situated on a sunny, south-facing slope in a tiny Hampshire parish. Knighton had at last bought the cottage that he promised Dorothea in 1809.

Chapter 5
Home, Sincerity and Affection

One of Knighton's neighbours in Hanover Square was the Reverend Sir Samuel Clarke Jervoise whose seat, which he did not particularly like, was Idsworth in Hampshire. Generations of local historians have studied the Clarke Jervoise family. In particular Dr K S Southam concentrated on the papers now at Hampshire Record Office while Richard Culpin has used sources both inside and outside Hampshire to tease a chronological narrative from centuries of documents. The accumulated research explains why, of all the quiet villages in early nineteenth-century England, Knighton chose the tiny parish of Blendworth in Hampshire. Moreover the appearance of Dorothea's sisters' married names in impersonal official records such as land tax and parish rates reveals a side of Knighton omitted from political histories and barely mentioned in the *Memoirs*. At Blendworth Knighton lived among people who had known him for twenty years or more, and he was there because an unnewsworthy but wealthy cleric went out of his way to secure him as a neighbour.

The Reverend Sir Samuel Clarke Jervoise was the youngest of three sons. The first, Thomas, was so eccentric that he was posthumously declared insane. The second, Robert, was supervised throughout his life. Samuel entered the Church. Born Samuel Clarke, he adopted an additional surname to inherit more money and, as Richard Culpin observes, in 1813 he was created a baronet for being 'a man eminent for family inheritance and estate and integrity of manners' – in other words, for being rich. Since 1809 Samuel had been contesting the will of his eldest brother, the eccentric Thomas, in a dispute that was not resolved until the 1820s. Thomas inherited the family estates in 1808 and immediately made a will that showed complete disregard for both primogeniture and Samuel. Under Thomas's will the family estates were to be sold at public auction and the proceeds divided between Samuel's children. Thomas died in 1809, a year after inheriting, by which time his eccentricities were said to have included hauling the contents of one house onto the lawn to make a bonfire and pulling down the staircase of another.

The Hampshire estates included huge areas of farmland, and as the case dragged on Samuel was seemingly out of step with the times in wanting to acquire them. He was belligerent, at one point describing the opposing counsel as 'a wicked and abandoned man'. When Samuel planned to confront his opponents with an ultimatum, his own legal adviser told him that his proposal was embarrassing. In September 1822 a surveyor reported that since the end of the war in 1815 Portsmouth had ceased to provide a reliable market for agricultural produce, and he recommended breaking up the estates before offering them for sale. The report was correct. Few people wanted farms, and the local press advertised farmhouses that were capable, at moderate expense, of being converted into residences fit for the reception of genteel families. In a first sale in 1820 the small lots sold well and Samuel lost them, while the large farms failed to find buyers. In the event, however, probably because of Samuel's influence, the farms were not divided, and after a final sale in 1823 Samuel, having sworn 'not to advance one sixpence beyond £70,000', paid more than £90,000. His subsequent actions suggest that he had all along decided that if anyone was going to divide up the farms into small, profitable plots, it would be him. Being 'eminent for family inheritance' he could afford to be patient.

Reverend Sir Samuel was the rector, or 'incumbent', of several livings. Livings are ecclesiastical parish jobs and at that time they could be bought, sold or inherited just like any other possession. They had a monetary value because they conferred benefits – hence the alternative name 'benefice'. These included somewhere to live, some 'glebe land' to farm or rent out, and tithes, which were property-based payments from parishioners. The living provided the means by which its incumbent could live. In return livings involved duties. These included an obligation to provide religious services, though not necessarily in person. Anyone with sufficient cash could buy a living and thereby become its 'patron'. A patron was entitled to 'present' the living to an ordained appointee of his or her choice, and many families bought livings to provide for ordained sons. If the appointee wished, he could fulfil the patron's obligation by paying a curate to conduct religious services.

One of the Reverend Sir Samuel's livings was Blendworth, the parish next to Idsworth. Although the Blendworth living was among the lots sold at the 1820 auction, new patrons could not exercise their presentation rights until existing incumbents were removed by resignation, death or disgrace. The Blendworth living changed hands but Reverend Sir Samuel remained in post. Much of the land that he hoped to acquire lay in Blendworth, and in the summer of 1818 he presented the Blendworth curacy to Knighton's nephew by marriage, the Reverend Charles Gower Boyles. Reverend Boyles was the only son of Dorothea's eldest sister, Mary, and her husband, Admiral Sir Charles Boyles. Admiral Boyles had died in 1816, bequeathing £10,000 in stock to his son. Nevertheless Reverend Boyles had to serve time as a curate if he wished to progress in his vocation.

Strong circumstantial evidence suggests that Samuel went out of his way to tempt Reverend Boyles to Blendworth. At some time between 1816 and 1819, the years in which Knighton was supplanting Bloomfield in George's affections, Samuel bought a farmhouse called Green Hook in the parish of Blendworth and let it to Reverend Boyles and his widowed mother, Mary. Reverend Boyles was a very different man from his predecessor, the Reverend John Coulthred. Ordained in 1771, Coulthred was appointed curate to Blendworth in 1813. On his journey to Blendworth to take up his curacy he lost his trunk, containing his valuables and papers. He never acquired a full living. The Blendworth parsonage – if Coulthred indeed got it, for Samuel may have let it – was what Samuel described as a 'cottage parsonage' with a thatched roof and casement windows. Explaining to the bishop why Boyles could not live there, Samuel described it as 'a very indifferent habitation'. The accommodation that Samuel provided for Boyles was a substantial farmhouse with land and outbuildings which Boyles soon bought outright.

At first it appeared that Samuel's success in gentrifying Blendworth with a well-educated curate and his widowed mother had served only to help his neighbours. Adjacent Green Hook was Blendworth Cottage, the home of John Hopper, a Royal Navy purser who had served at Trafalgar in 1805. Just north was Hook Cottage owned by James Charles Mottley, a newspaper proprietor and man of business from Portsmouth. A little further west was Blendworth House, home of a mysterious Welsh brewer with a mistress in Sussex. Knighton and his in-laws would buy all three before Samuel saw any more Devon money.

Blendworth House went to Seymour who, thanks to Boyles, knew the countryside on the Hampshire–Sussex border and, thanks to Knighton, was looking for a house within travelling distance of Portsmouth. Seymour was a good-humoured, attractive, talented Irish Protestant, who had joined the navy at twelve. He married James Hawker's third daughter, Jane – Jenny, or 'her dearest Ladyship' as he called her – in 1798, by which time he had twice been invalided home to England, once from the effects of the West Indies' climate and once after the amputation of most of his left arm. He eventually made his name and money in individual engagements with enemy vessels. By 1819 he was Captain Sir Michael Seymour, with an adequate though not excessive amount of capital with which to house himself and Lady Seymour and provide for his five – eventually six – sons and seven daughters.

Peace with France had reduced Seymour's income and opportunities, and now aged fifty he needed a permanent appointment. Although Knighton was a newcomer at Court, in the summer of 1819 he obtained for Seymour command of the *Prince Regent*, a new royal yacht based at Portsmouth, about ten miles from Blendworth. Seymour's biographer, his son Richard, acknowledged that although Seymour's record entitled him to the promotion, it was Knighton's influence that secured it. Seymour could live anywhere within travelling distance of Portsmouth and by the end of 1819 he had bought Blendworth House. Despite its dining and drawing rooms, library and conservatory, it was a modest home for a baronet. However Blendworth was proving attractive to Dorothea's sisters. Another sister, Elizabeth Osborn, soon came to Blendworth House with her husband. He died there in July 1820, but Elizabeth remained in the area. When in 1829 Boyles obtained a full living at a nearby village she rented his property, Green Hook. More importantly her son, Edward Osborn, moved to Blendworth after his ordination in 1829 to take up the curacy left vacant by Boyles' preferment.

Blendworth Cottage, advertised as a cottage ornée, went to the Knightons. A cottage ornée was originally a pretty miniature residence at which a family could take refreshment while touring their parkland, but by the 1800s it was a pretty miniature residence minus the parkland. Cottages ornées appealed to people who wished to live comfortably and respectably but without ostentation. Blendworth Cottage was surrounded by a lawn and shrubberies, had a summer house and partly-walled kitchen garden, a small farm to supply the household, and stabling and hay-producing fields for carriage horses. Two of Hopper's three wives died there and he had advertised it for sale several times without success, but it was exactly the sort of home to which Knighton had aspired in 1809. In May 1820, when Caroline and unpleasantness were expected, Knighton bought it. Half a mile away from Blendworth was Horndean, a post town where coaches to and from London changed horses, so Knighton was in easy contact with town. However the Knightons' move to Blendworth marked a deliberate separation of family from Court.

Whenever land around Blendworth Cottage came up for sale, Knighton bought it. On the morning of 17 May 1821 he called on Reverend Sir Samuel who was in town to consult his counsel and hopeful of an early settlement. After Knighton's visit Reverend Sir Samuel unburdened himself in a letter to his Hampshire solicitor. Most of the letter concerned his dealings with Thomas's trustees. However there was a further item worth mentioning and he added, 'Sir William has just left me, asked what news there was from Hants. I think silently he regrets not having bought Sarson's.' Reverend Sir Samuel was right. George Sarson was a Blendworth farmer. Mottley's family bought part of his land and later sold it on to Knighton. Mottley had been ambitious. He had acquired Hook Cottage by exchanging land with Thomas's trustees and in 1818 he had advertised it for sale. Although it was almost certainly a rebuild he described it as a new house, fit for the reception of a small family but requiring only a little expense to be easily converted into the residence of a gentleman. It failed to sell.

A month after Knighton's purchase from Hopper, Mottley readvertised Hook Cottage, which had by then acquired a striking similarity to Blendworth Cottage. Mottley pointed out its proximity to the estate lately purchased by Sir William Knighton, and indeed the intervening fields afforded each an unimpeded view of the other. Within a few years Knighton had secured privacy for Blendworth Cottage from the east by buying Hook Cottage and the fields attached to it, and he added to the cordon by buying from Reverend Sir Samuel a cottage that stood opposite Blendworth Cottage.

Northcote claimed that Dorothea lived the sad life of a widow because Knighton was so often away on George's business, but with Jane at Blendworth House, Mary and then Elizabeth at Green Hook, and her nephews and nieces around her, she was not alone. She also had her own three children. William was sent to the same preparatory school in Tavistock as his male Seymour cousins. Between 1822 and 1826 he attended Charterhouse, a London school for gentlemen's sons and part of a trust that provided almshouses for respectable men no longer able to work. After an unexplained gap of two years he attended Christ Church, Oxford between 1828 and 1831. He struggled with his studies, being 'turned down in his class' – held back a year – at Charterhouse, and at Oxford he asked Knighton for a private tutor. He obtained his degree, but a pass rather than honours.

The Knightons' daughters, Dora and Mary Frances, received at least part of their education from a governess, Jane Metzler, born in Frankfurt and first mentioned in the *Memoirs* as 'Mlle M' in December 1824. Mary Frances was christened ominously early, only five weeks after her birth, and passing references suggest that she was delicate. Britons in poor health often wintered abroad, and a popular destination was Nice. The British consular representative at Nice was an Italian, 'Peter' Lacroix. For a tip or a percentage he also acted as agent, broker and tour guide, and as a result he was not wholly popular with the British expatriates. Nevertheless the *Memoirs* referred to him with affection. There was also praise for Nice. Detained there in December 1824, Knighton enthused over its scenery and flora, telling Dorothea that kalmia that would cost fifteen or twenty shillings apiece in England grew by their thousands on the mountains, as did arbutus covered with fruit. He acted on his inclination. The circumstances are missing from the *Memoirs*, Aspinall's *Letters* or any published sources, but West Sussex Record Office holds a letter from Nice dated November 1827 in which Reverend Sir Samuel's eldest son, Jervoise, recalled that Knighton had said that he owned property there. Jervoise had spoken to Lacroix who had given a good account of that year's produce and promised to show him round. If the Nice property was a secret, it was an open secret.

Comparison of the *Memoirs*' version of Knighton's diary for February 1830 with its original at the Royal Archives shows that to protect the privacy of friends and family Dorothea edited entries concerning Knighton's private life. However his continued contact with his family in Devon was another open secret. Knighton and Dorothea witnessed Thamzin's marriage in December 1800, four months after their own. Thirteen months later, in January 1802, they buried their first child at St Andrew's churchyard at Bere Ferrers, not in Plymouth or Devonport. Knighton did not return to Devonport from the time he left in 1803 until 1832, two years into his retirement, but as a society physician though not yet a royal confidant he took Dora and William to Lockeridge to meet Dorothy. He last saw Dorothy in late summer 1817, when he was sufficiently established at Court for a messenger to be sent to Devon to tell him of McMahon's death. When Dorothy Toll made her will in February 1820, ten months before her death, her bequests reflected need rather than seniority. Knighton, her wealthiest child, received the smallest legacy of only one pound, but as her eldest son he was named first. Knighton's younger half-brother, John, received ten pounds but none of Dorothy's small portions of land. However three years later, in July 1823, John became Steward and Collector of Rents at Brighton. By then he was known as John Tolle, and as John Tolle he became Knighton's deputy at the Duchies of both Cornwall and Lancaster. John's will, made within three years of Knighton's death, reconciled Bere Ferrers and Blendworth, with bequests to his elder brother, James Toll, still farming at Lockeridge; to his widowed half-sister Thamzin; to William and Dorothea, the heir and widow of his late half-brother, and to Jane Metzler. The residue of John's estate went to Michael, whom he appointed his executor.

Knighton's will also remembered Jane Metzler, who was a valued member of the household. After his death she remained with Dorothea, and her own death in October 1847 was noted in *The Times*. However she was not one of the family. A letter of November 1832 from Sally Luscombe, the only one of Dorothea's sisters who remained in Devon, listed a pair of cuffs from 'Miss Mitzler' among presents sent from Blendworth to Devon. In contrast, family correspondence referred to the sisters by their surnames prefixed by 'Aunt'. Dorothea was 'Lady Knighton' or 'Aunt Knighton'. Knighton was 'dear Sir William'. Knighton's original diary of February 1830 referred to Dorothea as 'Lady Knighton'. However he began a letter to Sally Luscombe with 'My dear Sally', perhaps to soften his message, which was that he would do his utmost to secure posts for two of her younger sons, but could promise nothing. He omitted to mention that he had just recovered from a severe illness and was about to go abroad, but in a postscript he asked to be remembered to his friend John. This was Sally Luscombe's eldest son, aged midway between Michael and William, and probably one of the *Memoirs*' 'dear Johns'.

Although Knighton's original diary of February 1830 and the Luscombe correspondence record visits to and from Devon, the centre of family life remained Blendworth, and at eight o'clock on the morning of 22 June 1829 there occurred in Blendworth a wedding worthy of the romances about which Knighton had teased Thamzin some thirty years earlier. The handsome Captain Michael Seymour, son of Seymour and Jane, returned from duty on the Royal Navy's South America station to marry pretty, dark-haired Dora Knighton, whose hand he had sought before he left England and who had had barely two-and-a-half years in which to make her wedding preparations, with no female advice other than that of her mother, three aunts and seven cousins. The service was conducted by Charles Richard Sumner, Knighton's friend from Carlton House and by then Bishop of Winchester, at the tiny parish church of St Giles across the fields from Blendworth Cottage. The wedding had at last induced Knighton to buy some of the land for which Reverend Sir Samuel had held out for so long. Dr Southam, in his painstaking cataloguing of Clarke Jervoise accounts, noted that in March 1828 a tenant who farmed the fields north of Blendworth Cottage was compensated for loss of his crop on land that Reverend Sir Samuel had sold to Knighton. This was the site of Cadlington House, the future home of Dora and Seymour, named after the field on which it was built. The architect was probably Joseph Henry Good, a man of around Knighton's age who became architect for Brighton Pavilion and who carried out work for Knighton at Blendworth during the 1820s.

The Blendworth to which Knighton and his in-laws moved was changing. Hopper, who as a purser was perforce literate and numerate, had been one of its churchwardens, but only a decade or so earlier some churchwardens had made their mark on the vestry accounts. It was not a question of money. Knighton and Seymour would never be as wealthy as Reverend Sir Samuel, and the brewer from whom Seymour bought Blendworth House owned much other property. It was means and aspirations that had changed. John Pile of Hampshire Field Club has noted that after enclosure in 1816 Blendworth ceased to be a community hemmed in by its common land. Enclosure had created large blocks of unprofitable farmland, but there was a new market for homes for unemployed naval officers on half pay. Most were second, third or fourth sons. They had accumulated modest amounts of prize money with which to buy properties but would never have enough income to maintain large estates. They lived for hunting but would never keep a pack. They were educated, sociable and well travelled but could not entertain grandly.

Inside this world the homes of Knighton and his extended family formed a communal family estate. A lane ran yards from Blendworth Cottage and separated Cadlington House from its front garden, but otherwise boundaries were marked by planting and there were no hard boundary walls. Knighton was not the centre of this world. His in-laws had standing in their own right and their connections were naval, military and ecclesiastical. Family life at Blendworth was, like Dorothy's death, too private to be included in the *Memoirs* and is discernible only in precious vignettes. Writing to her cousin John Luscombe at some time before her marriage, Dora teased him about the beautiful Seymour girls who were then on a visit to Devon, and she hinted at a past flirtation with one in particular. Blendworth seemed very strange without them. John was nervous about his Confirmation, and Dora sympathised and wished him well. The weather at Blendworth was excessively hot, but they had had 'a very agreeable little *tea* picnic' – Dora did not explain why she underlined 'tea' – at a local beauty spot, Hayling Island, not returning home until eleven at night. That was the sort of party Dora liked best. A favourite clergyman was still at Blendworth and had given two beautiful sermons – one at Blendworth and another at nearby Catherington. Knighton's original diary for February 1830 recorded his attendance at morning service at Blendworth, and Edward Osborn, Edward's sister and Sally Luscombe coming to dine. When Sally Luscombe wrote her letter of November 1832 she was staying with the Boyleses. Knighton and Dorothea, and Dora and her 'two darlings' were the visitors. Dora had been 'much provoked' that geranium cuttings had been taken from flowering stalks, while Sally sent instructions about her grapes in Devon and was looking forward to a visit from the Plymouth Hawkers on her return home. Blendworth was a sanctuary of affection and decency whose existence sustained Knighton when he was far from home, tired, isolated and negotiating with people who appalled him. Writing from ancient castles, Parisian hotels and roadside inns, he asked Dorothea to kiss the children for him and tell them how often he thought of them. Even on his first trip to Hanover in 1821 he ended a letter, 'The bundle at Blendworth Cottage, amidst all my grandeur, are my only comforts.'

No matter how sensitive, secret or arduous Knighton's missions he always found time to buy presents and, to ensure that he was not forgotten and that his return was eagerly awaited, his letters home described the treasures he was bringing home. None had great monetary value. All were carefully chosen. For ten-year-old 'dearest W.', Knighton's visit to Hanover in 1821 promised artefacts from the Waterloo battlefield and perhaps, but not definitely, a gun. A European journey of 1,600 miles in the summer of 1824 to visit a dying man yielded a 'pretty cross' for Mary Frances and, for 'beloved William', some minerals that Knighton bought 'about six miles up the side of the Pyrenees'. Dorothea could look forward to 'valuable flower-seeds' from the garden at Herrenhausen. Although she regretted her husband's absences she recognised their horticultural possibilities. When Knighton accompanied the dying man to the south of France in the winter of 1824 he was briefed on seeds to be obtained in Paris and Nice. In the summer of 1829, on his way to conduct delicate negotiations with one of George's brothers, Knighton rose at six one morning to visit the botanic garden at Göttingen and arrange for rarities to be forwarded to Dorothea that autumn.

In November 1824, when Knighton was ordered abroad at a moment's notice for the third time in five months, he referred wryly to his '*agreeable situation*'. Subsequent journeys were equally unpredictable but mentally and physically more demanding, and his health soon began to falter. Dorothea believed that the illness that ultimately caused Knighton's death started early in 1827, but in March 1825 Knighton had sent a melancholy letter to Dora, then in her late teens and already a confidante, describing himself as 'tired and embarrassed', using 'embarrassed' in the sense being wholly or partially incapacitated by ill health. A month later he confessed to George Canning, then Foreign Secretary, that he would prefer to limit himself to his Privy Purse duties, which he could conduct from Blendworth, and come up to town purely to settle his accounts. Northcote believed that Dorothea missed Knighton but acquiesced to his absence because of the benefits that the family gained from his presence at Court. This was unlikely, for Knighton exercised his considerable patronage to obtain only modest benefits for his in-laws. However one of Northcote's anecdotes suggested that Knighton planned for the day when he could leave. In the summer of 1828 Knighton commissioned Northcote to paint a portrait of Walter Scott, one of George's favourite popular authors. The work was to be done discreetly, the painting was not to be exhibited and George was not to know of it. It was the sort of gift that Knighton might wish to have ready to soften the blow of his departure.

Benjamin Brodie wrote that Knighton came to regret entering George's household but was persuaded by Dorothea that it would be improper for him to resign while he still held George's confidence. Knighton inadvertently identified the problem in 1822 when he referred to Bloomfield as being part of George's family, a contemporary term for household. People walk out on their families, they abandon them or are cast out by them. They do not resign from them. When Knighton walked in the procession for George III's funeral as one of George's physicians, he was displaying not his own importance but that of the new King. Knighton was incorporated into royal pageantry and it was for George to dismiss him, not for Knighton to resign because the job no longer suited him. The woman whom George once dismissed as 'poor little soul' had grasped the essentials more firmly than had the man whom he called his 'dearest friend', and George's demands continued to summon Knighton from Blendworth.

CHAPTER 6
1822–1825: THE KING'S DEAR FRIEND

By 1823 Knighton was undertaking so much work for George that he resigned as physician-in-ordinary. Commands arrived by messenger and required Knighton to leave at once for wherever George was in residence. For most of the reign George's London home was Carlton House on the north-east corner of St James's Park. It had been his official residence since he became Prince of Wales in 1783 but in 1827 he had it demolished, intending to move to Buckingham House, the London home of his late mother, at the more secluded western end of the park. While Buckingham House was being refurbished George took temporary accommodation a few hundred yards west of Carlton House at St James's Palace. St James's Palace contained accommodation for the use of George's brothers but was no longer a royal family home, and repairs in the early 1820s reflected its official functions. When George left town his destination was usually the Royal Lodge in the grounds of Windsor Castle or the Pavilion at Brighton, but cotemporaneous with the transformation of Buckingham House into Buckingham Palace was the renovation of Windsor Castle. George died before Buckingham House was finished but he took possession of the completed Windsor Castle in December 1828. Once Knighton arrived at a royal residence he became part of the household, socialising, dining or working as required. He had his own rooms at Carlton House and the Pavilion, while the Royal Lodge and Windsor Castle had suites of guest accommodation to delay his return to Blendworth.

Although much of the money for refurbishment was voted by Parliament, Knighton's attention to detail was required as overseer of George's finances, and on his own initiative he travelled within Britain to inspect the estates that formed George's portfolios. In London he attended three Government offices. First, as Keeper of the Privy Purse Knighton had offices in the newly-created Ambassadors' Court, St James's Palace, with Thomas Marrable as his secretary. Secondly, as there was no Prince of Wales, George retained the income from the Duchy of Cornwall. As a result Knighton remained at the Duchy of Cornwall, initially as auditor and from 1823 as Receiver-General, and in these capacities he attended the Duchy of Cornwall offices in the east wing of Somerset House on the north bank of the Thames, opposite St Mary le Strand. Thirdly, Knighton became Receiver-General and then Vice-Chancellor of the Duchy of Lancaster, a portfolio of property and investments that provides income for the monarch. The Duchy of Lancaster had rooms at Somerset House but its main office was at Lancaster Place, within easy walking distance on the approach to Waterloo Bridge. Both Duchy offices were convenient for Coutts in the Strand, George's bankers.

As George's unofficial private secretary, Knighton undertook tasks that George feared to entrust to anyone else. To the anger of many contemporaries, Knighton also liaised between George and Government Ministers and discussed politics with George. Although George was a constitutional monarch, little could be achieved without his co-operation and three dilemmas caused him particular anxiety. The first was the conflict of interest created by his dual crown. As king of Hanover George was free to conduct his own foreign policy; as King of England he was required to consult his Ministers. The second was agitation for the reform of public life and Parliamentary representation. The third was pressure for Roman Catholic emancipation.

From the mid-1820s Knighton frequently travelled abroad on George's behalf, often at a moment's notice. These journeys were of three kinds. First were trips east to the German States, perhaps dropping south to Vienna, usually to conduct George's family business. Second were trips to the south of France in 1824 to visit the dying son of George's companion, Elizabeth Conyngham. Third were trips to Paris for confidential meetings with British diplomats about events that pre-dated George's reign. On any one of these trips Knighton might also, for reasons of convenience or confidentiality, personally deliver royal or Government correspondence. He either travelled non-stop by coach from London to Dover where he embarked for Calais, or he embarked from London direct for the Continent. Occasionally he mentioned crossing the Channel by steamboat which, independent of wind power, would have suited his urgency. Time permitting he stayed overnight in Calais at the Hotel Bourbon or at the more prestigious Hotel d'Angleterre, known as Dessin's after its proprietor, before resuming his journey. He travelled with a courier or, preferably, a reliable companion of his own choosing. In January 1829 he proposed to take 'Le Blanc', who was probably the younger William le Blanc, a lawyer from a London firm that had acted for George and for the Reverend Sir Samuel Clarke Jervoise. In June that year Knighton took William. He may also have travelled at some time with a certain 'Joseph', perhaps Joseph Henry Good, his Blendworth architect. Knighton considered himself an expert on accommodation in Europe and with easier times in mind noted establishments suitable for families.

The Europe through which Knighton travelled was a short-lived arrangement of states created at the Congress of Vienna in 1815 by the Allies who had defeated Napoleon – Britain, Prussia, Russia and Austria – and was intended to prevent a repeat of French expansion. The king and queen of the Netherlands, with whom George's suite dined at Brussels in 1821, ruled a country formed of Belgium and modern Holland, one large country being considered less vulnerable than two small ones. The Kingdom of Sardinia, enlarged to form a buffer on France's south-east border, comprised the eponymous island, Savoy and Piedmont in northern Italy, and the town of Nice and the city of Genoa on the Riviera. It was one of ten Italian states, so the wild kalmia and arbutus of Nice were growing in Italian and not French soil when Knighton described them to Dorothea. Vienna, which he visited in 1825, was the capital of an empire that included Milan and Venice and which was pre-eminent in a group of thirty-nine states, including Hanover, that called themselves the Germanic Confederation.

Knighton was frequently required in the German States because four of George's siblings, now middle-aged, lived in these territories.

His eldest sister, Charlotte, had married the king of Würtemberg, a south German kingdom, and was now its widowed queen dowager. Another sister, Elizabeth, was married to the landgrave, or hereditary ruler, of Hesse-Homberg, a German duchy between Hanover and Würtemberg. George's youngest brother, the popular and sensible Adolphus, Duke of Cambridge, was George's viceroy in Hanover. His youngest-but-two brother, the scandal-prone opponent of Roman Catholicism, Ernest, Duke of Cumberland, was George's deputy viceroy but lived mostly in Potsdam near Berlin, the capital of Prussia. Ernest's son, George, and Adolphus's son, George William, had German mothers and spent most of their lives in the German States but they were English princes and George, as their uncle and sovereign, wished to supervise their education. Of George's family in Britain, Knighton frequently liaised with Frederick, Duke of York, nearest in age to George and expected to succeed him as King, and William, Duke of Clarence, second in line to the throne.

The family of Elizabeth, Marchioness Conyngham, who was George's companion from 1820 until his death in 1830, also occupied Knighton's time at home and abroad. History has been ungenerous to Elizabeth Conyngham. By 1820 both she and George were in their fifties. Elizabeth had been a beauty in her youth and retained her looks but George was overweight and gross. Contemporaries lampooned the relationship, and the attention and gifts that George lavished on Elizabeth Conyngham ensured that she was his assumed mistress. Elizabeth seems to have tolerated her lot for the sake of her family. Her husband, Henry, an Irish peer, received a United Kingdom peerage, became a Privy Councillor and was given posts in George's household. His heir, also named Henry, suffered poor health, but the Conynghams' second son, Francis, received household and Government posts while their youngest son, Albert, was given a diplomatic post. It was the Conynghams who introduced George to Charles Richard Sumner, former tutor and tour guide to Henry and Francis, schoolmaster to Albert, and later a close friend to Knighton. After making Sumner's acquaintance George proposed his instant promotion from curate to canon.

1822–1825: The King's Dear Friend

The proposal nearly brought down the Government, so for propriety's sake Sumner became George's chaplain and librarian at Carlton House before receiving preferment.

It would be easier to write about the demands on Knighton, and easier to understand them, by dealing with them thematically. But that is not how Knighton experienced them. Aspinall's *Letters* and Dorothea's *Memoirs* record the events of his life in chronological order, and when his royal duties are placed end to end it becomes clear why they destroyed his well-being. In addition Knighton failed to gain political acceptance, and throughout his time at Court he was buffeted by three groups. One was a small, extreme Tory faction called the Ultras whom George gathered round him at the Royal Lodge during the first half of his reign and who initially tolerated Knighton as a useful outsider because of his influence with George. The most important Ultra was Arthur Wellesley who opposed political reform and supported strong monarchies. Other members were Arthur Wellesley's epistolary confidante, Harriett Arbuthnot, and her husband, Charles, a former diplomat and Treasury official who was by then in poor health. Foreign guests to the Royal Lodge included another of Arthur Wellesley's epistolary confidantes, Princess Dorothea Lieven, wife of the Russian ambassador to London and lover of Prince Metternich, the senior Austrian statesman who had hosted the Congress of Vienna. These were dangerous connections for George. After the Congress of Vienna three of the four Allies – Russia, Austria and Prussia – formed a Holy Alliance to ensure that in future Europe would be ruled by strong monarchies. George, monarch of the fourth Ally, was invited to join but could not because his foreign treaties had to be signed by Ministers from his Government. As king of Hanover however he was under no such restrictions and had an income with which to pursue foreign policy.

Overtly hostile to Knighton were the Whigs, who sought reform of Parliament and public life and who included Henry Brougham, counsel for Caroline. The Whigs hated George because he had abandoned them once he became Regent, and they despised Knighton for being a royal favourite. The final group were moderate Tories under Canning, the Foreign Secretary who fought a duel with the Secretary for War. For good measure George suspected that Canning had had an affair with Caroline. Canningites distrusted Knighton for being a sometime member of the Royal Lodge coterie. Even when he brokered an alliance between George and Canning he failed to win them over. Instead he lost the Ultras' support and confirmed the Whigs' suspicions. At one particularly beleaguered point of his life Knighton wrote that he belonged only to George, and in the absence of allies his claim seems true.

Once Knighton was gazetted as Keeper of the Privy Purse on 12 September 1822 he set about controlling George's debts, and at the end of October George issued an unprecedented notice. Tradesmen who were paid from the Privy Purse were warned to accept orders only if they were signed by Knighton, who was authorised 'to undertake the entire management' of George's private finances. As unofficial private secretary Knighton was the channel through which most people approached George. George's friends, family and members of his Government contacted Knighton if that was how George had started correspondence on a particular subject or if they believed that an initial approach to Knighton was more likely to succeed. Communications were also made solely to Knighton. In December 1822 George's physicians sent him 'a most confidential private document' alerting him to George's periodic attacks of breathlessness, irregular pulse and pains in the chest and left arm, and warning that life was sometimes 'extinguished suddenly' where such symptoms existed. If George was well enough to compose a letter but physically unable to write, Knighton wrote on his behalf, making it clear whether he was conveying George's sentiments or whether his letter was based on George's dictated words.

Knighton's abilities were not without limit. Aspinall's *Letters* contain a telling memorandum by John Scott, Lord Eldon, the Lord Chancellor. George told John Scott that he wished to make a will with the legatees' names left blank so that he could fill them in himself, but then named several of his legatees and told Scott how much he would bequeath to them. The problem was a residuary legatee whom George described as a friend but whom Scott inferred was Elizabeth Conyngham. Knighton was involved for two reasons. First, he was to be one of George's executors. Secondly, George had asked him to liaise with Scott. Knighton was of the same opinion about the residuary legatee. Without naming names he privately voiced his fears to Scott, but Scott was the finer diplomat. He explained that George could bequeath specified sums to private individuals, but it was not in the public interest for his residuary legatee to come from outside the royal family; the objection to Elizabeth Conyngham was not her relationship with George.

By the summer of 1823 George wanted to settle Knighton's unresolved status and he made it known to Robert Jenkinson, the Prime Minister, how much he would appreciate Knighton's admission to the Privy Council. Arthur Wellesley, who as Master General of Ordnance belonged to the Cabinet, agreed, as at present Knighton was privy to confidential affairs but not bound to secrecy. Jenkinson, whose sister Judith Schneid Lewis identifies as one of Knighton's former patients, declined to accede to George's wishes. According to Harriett Arbuthnot, Jenkinson claimed that Knighton was unsuitable because he had been accoucheur to half the ladies in London, while in a letter to Harriett's husband, Charles, Jenkinson warned of the '*dreadful publick evil*' of including 'such a man'. The matter dropped but it initiated speculation that Knighton was now Jenkinson's implacable enemy. However Knighton remained close to George, and in August 1823 he undertook his first Continental mission for George as part of the suite accompanying Cumberland and Prince George, then only three or four years old, to Europe. The *Memoirs* described a leisurely trip with time for sightseeing but with unspecified business in Paris.

The *Memoirs* and Aspinall's *Letters* show the remainder of 1823 taken up by a miscellany of parallel but unconnected royal concerns. The Duke of Clarence asked Knighton to convey his thanks to George for two kindnesses to his family. Knighton corresponded with Thomas Lawrence, now Sir Thomas and president of the Royal Academy, about one of many commissions from George. In mid-November 1823 the Conynghams' eldest son, Henry, who had been at Malvern Wells for the past six months because of ill health, wrote to thank Knighton for a cheering letter, and to say how much he enjoyed the repeated visits Knighton made at George's request, and how grateful he was for George's interest.

Royal finance remained important. On 2 December George received from George Harrison, Knighton's successor as auditor of the Duchy of Cornwall, £125,000 in cash, a loan from Rothschild & Sons of Frankfurt secured on George's Hanoverian income. On George's instructions Harrison had placed the money in three packets, each containing a specified sum. Knighton delivered one to the Duke of York, to whom George gave £50,000 to clear his debts. To Charles Arbuthnot, who in addition to suffering poor health may have incurred debts on behalf of the Crown, George gave £15,000. Of the remainder, £5,000 was to be 'put by as a fund for secret and collateral services connected with your Majesty's service', perhaps relating to George's Hanoverian diplomatic contacts, whose intelligence reports he failed to share with Canning, his Foreign Secretary.

So far there had been no hint of the sacrifices to health that Knighton would make on George's behalf. Lawrence's portrait of Knighton, finished in 1823 when Knighton was in his mid-forties, shows a man with a direct gaze and pleasant, even features. The corners of his mouth might or might not be about to turn upward into a discreet smile. Even allowing for flattery Knighton looks younger than his years. He was busy but not unpleasantly so. In January 1824 he received from the Earl of Lauderdale a recommendation that George should place a piece of lint steeped in myrrh under his false teeth, which were known to cause him pain, before he inserted them. The following month Knighton successfully conveyed George's wish that two young men, one of whom was a son of Seymour, be given studentships at Christ Church College, Oxford. George's right to bestow studentships was doubtful, but Knighton's letter implied that the awards were required by 'gracious commands'. George Colman, the examiner of plays, replied to Knighton's enquiry about a play that might be construed as promoting rebellion. The Duke of Clarence asked whether he could have a spare strip of land at St James's Palace for a kitchen. Bloomfield, who had been offered a post at Florence, said that he would accept it if he had to, but that he would lose money by it.

In late July 1824 Knighton embarked on the first of three journeys to the south of France necessitated by George's relationship with Elizabeth Conyngham. The connection is not at first obvious. On 9 August 1824 Knighton wrote home from St Jean de Luz, a French village near the Spanish border on the Atlantic coast, saying that he had just come from Barèges and that he would go back there in a few days. He would then proceed to Montpellier on the Mediterranean coast and return home via Paris. Knighton did not explain that Barèges was a Pyrenean invalid resort south of Lourdes. Instead he wrote that he was lodged with the maire of St Jean de Luz and would be travelling over the border into Spain by mule to finish some business. Knighton may have had some perfectly respectable reason for going to Spain. Alternatively his business may have been connected with the invasion of Spain in 1823 by France's restored monarchy, which George and the Ultras supported, to rescue neighbouring Spain from republicanism, which they opposed. At the same time Canning, the new Foreign Secretary, was seeking recognition of Spain's South American colonies as independent states against the wishes of George, who believed that recognition would undermine the status of all monarchies and encourage revolution.

Knighton's presence at Barèges is explained in Arthur Wellesley's letters to Harriett Arbuthnot of 2 and 3 September 1824. On 1 September Arthur Wellesley dined quietly at Windsor with Knighton and Elizabeth Conyngham's husband while George and the other guests were, according to Arthur Wellesley, 'on a junketting party'. Henry Conyngham was now in Barèges on his way to an uncle in Florence but Knighton doubted whether he was well enough to get there. Henry's father needed to go to Ireland where he had property, but when his business there was finished he intended to see Henry. For propriety's sake Elizabeth Conyngham did not wish to remain with George while her husband was away, but most of all she too wanted to go to Henry. Unfortunately George wanted to go with her under the pretext of his own poor health. Arthur Wellesley argued that if the public believed that George's true reason for going abroad was to be with Elizabeth Conyngham, they would conclude that the King had relinquished his duties. With the royal household abuzz with rumour, the hero of Waterloo acted quickly. To keep George in the country he prevailed upon Elizabeth Conyngham to forgo her visit to Henry. To enable her to stay at Court he dissuaded her husband from going to Ireland. George was placated and the constitution safe. In return for the Conynghams' compliance Knighton was immediately sent abroad to take Henry Conyngham from Barèges to Italy, and on the afternoon of 2 September he left Windsor for Calais and a second journey to the south of France.

After travelling non-stop for three days and nights Knighton reached Paris where he was delayed, after which he then travelled a further three days non-stop. On 9 September 1824 Knighton arrived in Tarbes, a Pyrenean town north of Barèges and Lourdes. His journey was attracting attention. The next day he wrote to Dora rather than to Dorothea, explaining that the police were less likely to open a letter to Miss Knighton than one to Lady Knighton. He then described the house in which he was lodged, the hour at which he would depart and his plan to travel via 'the mountains' to the Mediterranean coast. Four days later he wrote to Dora from Toulouse, saying that both his letters to her would be opened and that he would write to dearest mama when he crossed the Alps. True to his word on 21 September he wrote to Dorothea from Toulon, midway between Montpellier and Nice on the French Mediterranean coast. He told her that he would be travelling east for only a few more days, after which he would go as fast as possible to Paris. He ended the letter, 'I shall say no more', adding that in a minute or so it would be read by the police.

If the French police read on they would learn only that Dorothea was to kiss Dora and Mary Frances and send Knighton's love to William, and that Knighton hoped that they would all spend a pleasant Christmas together. Aspinall's *Letters* however point to trouble at Nice, for in October 1824

1822–1825: The King's Dear Friend

Canning informed George that Lacroix's duties at Nice had been exceptionally difficult. Canning did not explain the circumstances but they are hinted at in a biography of George Canning by his private secretary, Augustus Granville Stapleton. Stapleton pointed out that by enlarging the Kingdom of Sardinia the Congress of Vienna had deprived the Genoese of their independence and placed them under the control of their enemies. Knighton's final surviving letter from the trip was written the following day, 22 September, from Fréjus, midway between Toulon and Nice. He was home by mid-October. In his absence Arthur Wellesley and Harriett Arbuthnot had exchanged epistolary gossip about Knighton's alleged ambition for an English peerage. With unabashed aristocratic prejudice Wellesley admitted that Knighton's services were worth ten times more than Bloomfield's but preferred him to remain 'the Barber' – the Ultras' alternative nicknames for Knighton were 'the man-midwife' or 'the accoucheur'. Neither peerage nor Privy Councillorship, wrote Arthur Wellesley, would make Knighton anything in 'Society'.

Knighton made one final journey in 1824. On 1 December George Colman called on Knighton at Carlton House but was told that Knighton was 'in the country' and that his date of return was 'uncertain'. Knighton was in fact on his way to Calais. He had been ordered abroad at a moment's notice and the previous evening, 30 November, he had written to Dorothea from Dover to say that he was waiting for a storm to abate before he could cross. The *Memoirs* omitted the reason for the visit but it was given in Charles Sumner's biography, published forty years later when the circumstances were no longer controversial. Sumner and Knighton were to go to Nice to be with Henry Conyngham who was now beyond all doubt dying. The journey from Calais took them eight days. With little prospect of Christmas at home, on 13 December Knighton wrote to Dora and William, explaining that the letter was for all but that he wished his two eldest children 'to have a joint letter as a little Christmas keepsake'. This was the letter in which Knighton described kalmia and arbutus growing wild, with the hotel table decorated with roses, violets, jonquils and jasmine from its garden. He wrote that his movements would be partly determined by 'contingent circumstances' and that he was constantly moving. Sumner stayed with Henry Conyngham who died on 27 December.

Knighton had left Nice on 20 December and in January 1825 he passed through Paris without paying a courtesy visit to the British ambassador. It was not the only unexplained aspect of the trip. On 13 January 1825, a month after Knighton wrote his 'Christmas keepsake' letter from Nice, George received from him £20,000 to be placed in a secret account at Coutts – the receipt from George to Knighton in Aspinall's *Letters* referred unambiguously to 'our secret account'. There is no proof of what George intended to do with the money but he had not ruled out threatening his Government. Aspinall's *Letters* contain a draft memorandum in Knighton's handwriting dated 27 January 1825 from George to Jenkinson about the King's Speech that Jenkinson would write for George to read at the opening of Parliament in early February. George was angry that he would be required to announce his Government's intention to recognise Spain's former colonies as independent states, a development that he believed would encourage revolution and precipitate a fresh European war. In the closing paragraphs of the memorandum George wrote that if the policy were pursued further he would 'feel himself justified in taking such measures as the Government [would] be ye least prepared to expect'. Whatever the measures were, George now had a fighting fund with which to finance them.

In the event George did not attend the opening of Parliament and the speech was read on his behalf. However his demands on Knighton continued. On the night of Tuesday, 15 March 1825 George wrote to Knighton from Windsor asking him to visit as soon as possible to settle several 'little matters ... of various natures, pecuniary as well as domestick' that had arisen. He was probably referring to an annuity that he wished to arrange for his nephew George, Cumberland's son. Ten days later Knighton was newly-arrived in Frankfurt on his way to Potsdam, having crossed Belgium and France in severe weather accompanied only by a German courier on the outside of the carriage. Cold, lonely and tired, he showed the first signs of the depression that would accompany his physical illness, writing that his 'elasticity' was passing fast and that he would soon be a shadow of his present self. Meanwhile at home a constitutional crisis was in the making and Knighton would be called upon to avert it.

Chapter 7
1825–1829: A New Friend

The problem was the acrimony between Canning and George, which is described in detail in the works on Canning by Harold Temperley and Wendy Hinde. George and Canning had many reasons to dislike each other, but by early 1825 the most serious was their disagreement about Spain's former South American colonies. Canning wanted Britain to recognise the colonies as independent states. George did not, and to undermine Canning he had indulged in what Knighton later described as 'continental gossipings' with European statesmen equally opposed to recognition. As a result of these differences George denigrated Canning in public and failed to show him diplomatic reports that he received in his capacity as king of Hanover, although in December 1823 George had requested and received from Canning a spare key to the Foreign Office boxes for Knighton's use. Canning at first suspected, and then obtained proof, that George was trying to conduct his own foreign policy independently of his Government and in breach of the constitution. By spring 1825 Canning was in a position to expose George, who looked to Knighton to save him.

In April 1825 Canning became ill. George seized the pretext to send Knighton to enquire after the Foreign Secretary's health, and immediately after the meeting Canning dictated a record of the conversation to his secretary. According to this account, Knighton assured Canning that George now realised that his misgivings over Canning's South American policy were unfounded and had relinquished his independent diplomacy. Further, Knighton placed himself at Canning's disposal to facilitate future relations between monarch and Foreign Secretary. It was an alliance between a man whose mother had sold butter and eggs at Plymouth market and a man whose mother had been an actress. Like Dorothy, Canning's mother had been widowed young. However as a gentleman's daughter, not a farmer's daughter, she had lacked skills with which to earn a living and in desperation had gone on the stage. As a result of intervention by the farmer's son, George now showed the actress's son all Hanoverian correspondence and declined to see foreign diplomats unless Canning was present. Hanoverian diplomats were informed that Britain was forbidden by its constitution to make agreements that compelled it to defend foreign governments against rebellious subjects. George had put aside his sympathies for the French attempt to save Spain and for a Europe ruled by a Holy Alliance of conservative monarchs.

The farmer's son spent the summer of 1825 on routine business. Several times that year Walter Scott used his acquaintance with Knighton to bring his latest projects to George's attention. In June the British Minister at Berlin bought statues and bracelets on Knighton's behalf. In August the Lord Chamberlain, the most senior royal household official, congratulated Knighton for paying off expenditure at Brighton. Thomas Lawrence reported from France on a portrait commissioned by George. In September Knighton wrote to Dora expressing his pleasure that she enjoyed reading and telling her that he found her letters delightful. None survives, but they seem to have been of the thoughtful kind that Knighton exchanged with Letitia Treby. Writing late at night after several days of headaches, he was subdued and tired. A mutual friend had died only a few days ago, prompting him to speculate on his own mortality. Tomorrow he would try to visit the widow. Though Knighton did not tell Dora, he was also about to visit Robert Gooch who was in declining health and unable to work.

By late October Knighton's health had improved, but he was about to depart on a journey of at least a month and was dreading it. His task was to accompany Albert Conyngham, Elizabeth Conyngham's youngest son, to Vienna. Through his new friend, Canning, George had arranged for Albert to be appointed attaché to Henry Wellesley, who was by then ambassador at Vienna and to whom Knighton was to explain George's wish that Albert be given a salaried post as a first step to promotion. George was so sensitive about the project that Knighton's absence was to be concealed, but once abroad concealment was abandoned. They travelled by day and spent the nights at inns with no back-to-back travelling, and Knighton made a detour to visit George's sister Elizabeth and her husband, the landgravine of Hesse-Homburg. He was back in England by 3 December 1825 when he sent belated wedding congratulations to Richard Wellesley, explaining that he had only just returned. In private he took steps to show that he was more than George's 'dear friend', with the result that in December two articles by him appeared in the Tory *Quarterly Review*. The *Review* consisted of critiques of one or more works on a common subject crafted into lively, readable pieces that were either popular or topical – Knighton wrote on the cause of Napoleon's death and the likelihood that plague was contagious. Reviewers had token anonymity and the *Review* was not a medical journal, but its standing was sufficient to remind everyone that Knighton could speak with authority on medical subjects.

Routine details remained Knighton's responsibility. In January of the New Year, 1826, George thanked him for expediting work at Windsor Castle and Buckingham House and for soothing the feelings of the Buckingham House architect, John Nash, and requested that a complete set of Handel's works be sent to the king of Prussia. A radical, antiquarian and publisher, Sir Richard Phillips, financially embarrassed, wrote to say that he possessed various curios, including a lock of hair that George had once sent to a mistress, and asked whether George would like to buy them. George was, Phillips suggested, under an obligation to him from the McMahon era. In March Canning sought Knighton's help in getting George to return Foreign Office boxes and sign documents. In April Knighton's powers at the Duchy of Lancaster were increased and he became directly responsible to George for making its management more like that of a private estate and, by implication, less like that of a Government office.

Knighton was still required to travel abroad, and on Monday, 3 July 1826 he left England for Paris and Berlin. He was accompanied by fifteen-year-old William, and Dorothea and Dora were to join them in Paris on their return from Berlin. It is tempting to conclude that his family was a decoy. Knighton's mission was one of extreme sensitivity and lies at the heart of Frances Wilson's biography of Sally Douglas's rival, Harriette Wilson, which disentangles the hints and allusions in official correspondence in the Granville papers at The National Archives and in Aspinall's *Letters*. The previous year Harriette Wilson had published her memoirs in serial form. She had earlier advised her former lovers that for a set sum she would omit their names, and many prominent men were believed to have bought themselves out. She was now living in France threatening further revelations that were, in the words of Frances Wilson's chapter heading, causing 'Panic at the Palace'.

According to the *Memoirs* Paris was merely a stopover on the way to Berlin. According to the Granville papers at The National Archives, however, Knighton had important business there. He arrived on the morning of Wednesday, 5 July and wrote immediately to the ambassador, Granville Leveson-Gower, Lord Granville, asking permission to visit as soon as possible to deliver letters from Canning and George. Canning's letter spoke of a matter that was causing 'great disquietude' in a certain quarter. George's letter asked Leveson-Gower to communicate with Knighton, whom he introduced as a 'Confidential Friend', upon a subject about which George was 'most deeply anxious'. On the evening of 6 July Knighton wrote to Leveson-Gower asking whether, if the French Director of Police declined to comply with a proposal that was to be made to him, he might nevertheless agree to place the individuals in question under police surveillance to reassure 'those at home, who are so anxious on the subject'. No names or events were mentioned. On 7 July Knighton and William left Paris for Berlin via Frankfurt where Knighton wrote to Mary Frances, asking her to give his love to Dorothea and Dora if they had not already left for Paris, and repeating details of the accommodation he had reserved for them. The *Memoirs*' account ended in Berlin, where Knighton met Prince George's tutor and took William to the Potsdam gallery and the palaces of Sans-Souci.

Knighton was back in Britain by mid-August, when he received from Jenkinson a letter that reflected the changed relations brought about by his approach to Canning. Jenkinson was glad that Knighton's visit to Berlin – he did not say what it was about – had been satisfactory, and invited Knighton to dine and stay overnight at his country home where he would meet Canning. However the subject that in July had caused such anxiety was not yet resolved. In September Knighton returned to Paris, this time with a letter from George to Canning, who was in France for discussions with Charles X, the new king of France. Not wishing to draw attention to himself, Knighton asked Leveson-Gower to give the letter to Canning, and to do so discreetly. Knighton was back in England by late September, when Arthur Wellesley told Harriett Arbuthnot that George drank spirits 'morning, noon and night', became agitated as a result and then needed huge doses of laudanum to calm down. In early October 1826 George sent Knighton to Paris with another letter to Canning, in which he said that he was suffering *'increased anxiety'* [George's italics] 'on a subject which need not be nam'd'. Finally, in a desperate letter to Knighton in late October 1826, George named the 'subject' as Harriette Wilson.

As Frances Wilson observes, only the deaths of those involved would put an end to the matter, and for the time being it was eclipsed by other concerns. Routine correspondence continued. One of George's physicians-in-ordinary asked Knighton to tell George of his election to the Royal Academy of Sciences in Paris and the promotion of his youngest son, for whom George had found an army commission. Walter Scott approached Knighton about a job for Scott's younger son, Charles, perhaps something 'in the diplomatic line'. Canning knew of Scott's wishes and, about to meet him for dinner, had already asked Knighton for advice on 'his Majesty's gracious interest in the young man's favour'. When Knighton wrote to William on 21 November he said how much he was looking forward to Christmas. He did not reveal that he had just soothed relations between Jenkinson, George and the Duke of York. The Government had agreed with George to neither oppose nor promote Roman Catholic emancipation. However the Duke of York, George's successor, believed that this policy would compromise the coronation oath to uphold the Church of England,

and had approached Jenkinson about his fears. The advice of Jenkinson and Arthur Wellesley was to do nothing to cause a crisis – in other words, to do nothing. This course was, Knighton advised George, 'exactly in unison' with George's wishes. He encouraged George to believe that, for the present at least, there would be no further trouble 'on this anxious & painful subject'.

Knighton's prediction was correct. On 5 January 1827 the Duke of York died. George wished his brother's remains to be placed as close as possible to those of their father, George III, so on 18 January, at George's command, Knighton went to St George's Chapel at Windsor Castle and descended by torchlight into the royal family's vault to choose the final resting place. In a letter to Dora two days later he described the unforgettable and near-religious experience of walking deep in the earth among the coffins of his late King and Queen and their family. Knighton assured Dora he would be spared the funeral in St George's Chapel that night. Instead he would remain with George, who was too unwell to attend. Nevertheless Knighton did attend the funeral and was one of the mourners who, chilled to the bone, later became ill.

In private Knighton and Dorothea had cause for celebration, for Dora was about to become engaged to her cousin Michael, the son of Seymour and Jane. However when Dorothea compiled the *Memoirs* she remembered early 1827 as the time when the disease that eventually killed Knighton started to become apparent. In February he became severely ill, with continued colds leading to what he called 'embarrassment about the heart'. Other casualties of York's funeral were Canning, who caught rheumatic fever, which can kill or leave the sufferer with a weakened heart, and Jenkinson, whose already frail health was further damaged. On 17 February Jenkinson suffered an incapacitating stroke, and Croker recorded that despite Knighton's ill health Arthur Wellesley and Charles Arbuthnot called the same day at Hanover Square to discuss how best to break the news to George. Soon afterwards Knighton left for the Pavilion where he again became seriously unwell. By early March he had recovered enough to travel, but he returned to London only to become ill again. Around this time he sent an affectionate but melancholy letter to Dora. She was, he wrote, one of his 'principal comforts'. His evenings at Hanover Square were 'lonely and silent' but he kept himself occupied. After attending church he had visited a friend, the painter David Wilkie, whose company had done him good. When Knighton was unwell he became pompous, and he told Dora he could not sit down to talk with 'common minds'. He ended the letter by saying that he would have a busy day tomorrow.

If Jenkinson failed to recover George would have to choose a new Prime Minister. It was not a free choice, for by convention the man he chose must be acceptable to Parliament and command sufficient support to form a Government. Thereafter royal prerogative ceased. George could not subsequently tell the Prime Minister or his Government what to do, so he ascertained intentions in advance. There were three possibilities, all Tories, and the deciding factor was their attitude to Roman Catholic emancipation. Canning believed that emancipation was desirable, Arthur Wellesley reluctantly accepted that it was necessary and Robert Peel, then Home Secretary, opposed it.

Canning, still far from well, expressed his pleasure that George and Knighton were feeling better and, behaving as though he were already Prime Minister, enclosed for George a report of a parliamentary debate. Charles Arbuthnot wrote plaintively to remind Knighton of their once close working relationship and to solicit Knighton's support for Arthur Wellesley. A Government whip sent Knighton a report on George's options. On the morning of 26 March George and Knighton had a long and detailed discussion, and George finally acted to end speculation. That night he wrote to Knighton, thoughtfully instructing the messenger not to call before five o'clock the next morning, and on 28 March Arthur Wellesley told Harriett Arbuthnot that Knighton had visited Jenkinson's wife to advise her that her husband was to be replaced. On 6 April George wrote to Knighton telling him to take care of himself 'for all our sakes', with the oblique command that he was not on any account to think of stirring until the following morning. Little or no advance had been made amidst what George described as 'almost unravelable perplexities'. However on 10 April George commanded Canning to form a Government.

Knighton had long been lampooned by cartoonists, but he now began to attract more influential critics. An early conflict was with Arthur Wellesley. The Duke of York's response to George's generosity of 1823 was to incur new debts. Only Knighton and Harrison knew of the £50,000 gift, and as a result George was publicly criticised for not settling his late brother's debts. In late May 1827, in an attempt to reduce the criticism of George, Knighton divulged to Arthur Wellesley the extent of George's financial help to his siblings, only to be told by Wellesley that he should not have committed such information to paper. There were also tensions with George, who in early June instructed a household official whom Knighton disliked to convey royal dissatisfaction with works at Windsor – George's bath was not yet completed, a floating bridge had sunk and, according to George, the whole Office of Works needed reorganising.

Nevertheless Knighton remained influential. In June Walter Scott sent for George's attention a publication from a society of which he was president and used the covering letter to invoke a promise by Knighton to help Charles, who had now taken his degree. Northcote, describing himself as 'illuminated' by association, explained that people asked him to approach Knighton on their behalf. He then listed half a dozen requests for posts or money, placing an exclamation mark after each one. Knighton was less sceptical. The petitioners' names are omitted, but one was an author who wished his brother to be made a pensioner of Charterhouse, whose governors always included the monarch. Subsequent correspondence identifies the writer as William Godwin, a novelist, radical and former Christian with whom Knighton had nothing in common save friendship with Northcote. By early July Godwin's brother was provided for.

Not all difficulties were so easily resolved. At the end of July Canning visited the Royal Lodge, and afterwards George confided to Knighton that the Prime Minister appeared ill. At George's command Knighton travelled to town and saw Canning, who said that he had a cough and felt tired, like an old man, but that all he needed was some rest. Canning was staying with friends at Chiswick, just outside London, and Knighton promised to visit him there the following day. In the meantime he took the precaution of sending for a respected physician. As promised Knighton called at Chiswick the next day, Wednesday, 1 August, and although he was not treating Canning he asked him a few questions. Did Canning have a pain in his side? Yes – Canning had been in pain for some days and was unable to lie on his side. Was there any discomfort in the shoulder? Yes – Canning had suffered rheumatic pains in his shoulder for some time. Knighton, who had started his medical training more than three decades ago, had to tell Canning that the cause of the pain was not rheumatism but liver disease. He sent for three further physicians to attend Canning, probably because he foresaw that official bulletins would have to be issued, but not until after Canning's death did these details appear in the press. By the weekend Canning was deteriorating fast and Knighton visited nearly every day, presumably reporting to George between times. By the afternoon of Tuesday, 7 August hope of recovery was abandoned. Canning died the following day. George swiftly appointed one of Canning's supporters, Frederick John Robinson, Lord Goderich, as the new Prime Minister on the understanding that his Government would continue Canning's policies.

During Knighton's last years at Court he became a trusted facilitator rather than an intimate. The Granville archive shows Knighton visiting Leveson-Gower in Paris to apprise him of changes in the Government since Canning's death. However Arthur Aspinall discovered a further reason for Knighton's visit. The following account is based on an appendix to the *Letters*.

On 2 September 1827 the Foreign Secretary, John William Ward, Lord Dudley, wrote to Leveson-Gower. Leveson-Gower had, Ward wrote, just received a visit from a '*great person* in the State'. However, Ward continued, the outcome of that person's journey was of considerable importance to a '*still greater person*'. A fortnight later Aspinall found Knighton at Aix-la-Chapelle in the Prussian Rhine Province near the border with modern Belgium. Knighton's first task was to deliver letters from George and Ward to Charles Bagot, the British ambassador to The Hague. Knighton would then continue to Berlin. Elizabeth Fox, Lady Holland, wrote that his mission was to arrange a marriage between two royal cousins – George, Prince of Cumberland, and Princess Victoria, daughter of the late Duke of Kent – which, she believed, would make Prince George the future sovereign. However Aspinall chose not to explain why Knighton was going to Berlin. Events elsewhere were far more interesting.

After meeting Knighton, Bagot sent a secret agent to Chimay in Belgium near the French border where Harriette Wilson was living with a man known as Colonel Rochfort. She was to be warned that everything she did was known, and that unless she pledged to discontinue directing 'annoyances' against 'a quarter which she would perfectly understand' she and her immediate acquaintances would suffer 'inconveniences'. When the agent arrived Harriette was away from home and, according to Rochfort, would not return until the following summer. In October she wrote to Bagot, describing what it was that she had in her power to reveal and stating her terms for silence. Bagot forwarded her letter to Ward but not to Knighton, believing that Knighton's 'employers' would be distressed if they realised that Bagot knew its contents. Ward agreed that to have shown the letter to Knighton would have provoked 'unnecessary irritation', and he observed that the person who was suffering most was blameless but was 'wounded through the sides' of those to whom he was attached. Ward continued, 'What letters those of the young gentleman, and what a specimen of discretion of a person at that very moment filling a situation of the highest confidence!' Ward did not name names, but the 'specimen of discretion' was undoubtedly Elizabeth Conyngham and the 'young gentleman' was one of Harriette's former lovers, John Ponsonby, who as a younger man had broken his engagement with the first woman and the hearts of both. Harriette had acquired letters exchanged long ago between Elizabeth Conyngham and Ponsonby and regarded them as insurance for her old age. Bagot and

Ward were inclined to pay the modest sums she asked for their suppression. Knighton was not. Ward admitted to Bagot that Harriette had been bribed in the past, though it is not clear whether he was referring to payments by former lovers to buy themselves out of her memoirs or to an arrangement connected with her current demands. Ironically the letters were not secret. Ward wrote that he had already been shown them in circumstances that he would not divulge but which he said would make an amusing tale. Nowhere did the correspondence mention that both Ward and Leveson-Gower had featured in Harriette Wilson's memoirs, though as buffoons, not lovers. By early November the consensus was that for the time being she should be ignored.

The remainder of Knighton's year was filled with unconnected issues. In early November the press reported that George wished to replace Knighton, and a month later Knighton wrote to reassure Dorothea that rumours that he and George had quarrelled were 'newspaper tricks' about which he and George had been laughing heartily only a few minutes since. At the beginning of December a relieved and grateful Scott, who two weeks earlier had feared that Canning's death would hinder Charles's prospects, reported that Charles was to be found a Foreign Office post. Knighton spent Christmas 1827 at home, but on 30 December George wrote plaintively to ask Knighton to attend at Windsor no later than 2 January 1828. Only Knighton, wrote George, could crush the 'host of vipers and hornets' that George believed was out to sting him both in person and through those dear to him. Aspinall was unable to transcribe George's explanation because the next page was missing, but the parallel with Ward's observation was in any case misleading. George's immediate problem was Robinson's failure to keep the Government intact. On 8 January Robinson resigned. The next day George appointed Arthur Wellesley.

Knighton was by then at the Royal Lodge, paying Privy Purse pensions and finishing his accounts. On 18 January, after his return to London, he sent a succinct, fatherly letter to William, who was about to go up to Oxford. William was at an age when the mind was vulnerable to 'corporeal influence' but, Knighton advised, sobriety would save him much inconvenience while a 'Christian scheme of morality' would ensure that all would go right. His advice was optimistic. The same day Elizabeth Fox told her son that Knighton, Rothschild and John Nash, then George's architect at Buckingham House, belonged to a small group of people who were 'the real ministers in the interior closet' and pulled the strings of their 'puppets' – she included Nash because money spent on royal buildings was allegedly misappropriated from elsewhere. Three days later Knighton warned William not to believe anything to his father's dishonour that might appear in the press or be insinuated in Parliament. Knighton belonged only to the King. At the end of January George, no doubt aware of the rumours, wrote to say that he was always pleased to see Knighton who was to visit whenever he wished. On 18 February the predicted attack was made. In a Commons debate a radical Member, Thomas Duncombe, informed the House of a 'secret influence behind the throne'. This 'invisible' and 'incorporeal' person controlled patronage and sudden ministerial changes –- by implication, the fall of Robinson's Government – and was linked to a 'master of unbounded wealth' – by implication, the banker Nathan Rothschild of Frankfurt – who was using his money to dominate Europe. When Duncombe concluded by trusting that the Prime Minister and Home Secretary would no longer allow the Crown's patronage 'to be operated upon by the prescriptions of a physician' the allusion to Knighton was unmistakable, and someone laughed. It was perhaps no coincidence that on the same day the Chancellor of the Duchy of Lancaster sent kind words, congratulating Knighton on his management of the Duchy and saying that he was loath to hold further Duchy council meetings until Knighton returned.

The previous evening Knighton had written George a comforting letter of good news about work on the royal homes, with assurances that George Harrison was a capable substitute for himself. Knighton was about to go abroad to end a scandal created nearly forty years ago. His distaste for this particular royal duty was so intense that Dorothea chose not to edit it from the *Memoirs*. The purpose of his trip however could under no circumstances be included.

By 1790 George, York and Clarence, George III's eldest sons, then in their twenties, had been in debt. Badly advised by cronies and officials and unable to distinguish between credit and income, they had sought concurrent loans of up to £300,000. Most loans involved four parties. George, York and Clarence, acting together, were the borrowers, and an agent or banking house was the lender. The third party was formed of individual investors from whom the lender raised the loan. The fourth party were trustees acting for both the borrowers and the lender. In a successful transaction the borrowers signed a bond acknowledging receipt of the loan from the lender and agreeing terms for repayment even though they had not yet received any money. The trustees held the bond in escrow while simultaneously receiving money from the lender, either in instalments or as a lump sum. Once the trustees had received the full amount of the loan from the lender, they gave the money to the borrowers and released the bond to the lender. Some schemes, in which the loan would be repaid when one of the borrowers became King, were potentially treasonable because they depended on George III's death. Others, in which the loan was raised on the Continent, were, like the Fitzherbert marriage, unwise and illegal for they too required George III's permission.

A full account of the episode that caused Knighton such distress awaits detailed research in the French Archives Nationales, but there are enough English-language sources to explain his difficulties. One is Aspinall's *Letters*; another is an anonymous pamphlet of 1814 entitled *The Royal Criterion* which is confirmed by other accounts in all but one aspect; a third is Foreign Office correspondence from the early 1820s and the Granville archive, both held at the National Archives. Fourthly, an article by Albert Goodwin, based on research in the Archives Nationales, examines the lender's subsequent career. While these sources fail to establish the facts beyond all reasonable doubt, they establish perceptions of the episode, and it was perceptions that created Knighton's difficulties.

In June 1790 George, York and Clarence had signed a bond with Jean Jacques de Beaune, an entrepreneur of uncertain nationality who was based at Union Court in the City. De Beaune would lend them £100,000, secured by unlimited liability on all their present and future assets, with interest payable from July and capital after a set period. He was authorised to subdivide the main bond into smaller bonds of £100 and sell them to individual investors who would also receive interest immediately and repayment after a set period. If he defaulted, George, York and Clarence would honour his liability to the small investors. De Beaune received a notarial copy of the bond to use as credentials so that he could raise the £100,000. Meanwhile the original was deposited with the trustees, London bankers Ransom, Morland and Hammersley, who awaited remittances from him.

Alone of all the accounts, *The Royal Criterion* claimed that in October 1790 de Beaune made a part payment of nearly £40,000 worth of diamonds which he sent via a French intermediary from Paris to Ransom, Morland and Hammersley, and which were later sold in the City. However the following month, on Thomas Hammersley's advice, George, York and Clarence cancelled the bond on the grounds that they had received nothing. Meanwhile in revolutionary France nervous savers bought de Beaune's £100 bonds in the belief that an investment backed by the British royal family was completely secure. They were mistaken. In 1792 France was drawn into wars with hostile Continental monarchies and in February 1793 it declared war on Britain, by which time the enterprising de Beaune was supplying artillery to the French army. Having received no interest from George, York and Clarence, de Beaune had paid little or none to the individual investors, many of whom fled the Terror for London where, they believed, they would be reimbursed. In response George's advisers denied responsibility, hinted darkly and invoked the law.

According to *The Royal Criterion*, twenty-seven foreign investors who had asked for their money, including a Swiss who obtained a legal opinion in his favour, were deported under the newly created Alien Act and disappeared or were guillotined. De Beaune, repeatedly accused of profiteering by the French government, was guillotined for treason, allegedly after the secretary at the British embassy in Paris colluded with the intermediary and assisted the prosecution by pointing out, quite correctly, that the legal jargon of the notarial copy described George III as King of Great Britain, France and Ireland. English investors also lost their money, and Hammersley was said to have intimidated one by alleging that George intended to prosecute them all for conspiracy.

For three decades royal advisers maintained that George, York and Clarence had received not a farthing from de Beaune whose bonds were therefore fraudulent and of no value; individual investors could, it was argued, have protected themselves by making the necessary enquiries. Nevertheless as late as March 1821 Charles Stuart, British ambassador in Paris, reported that de Beaune's bonds formed the basis of a 'Multitude of fraudulent money dealings' and that 'unwary Persons' bought them for eighteen or twenty per cent of their face value. Stuart, one of a new generation of diplomats, suggested a different tactic. First, the press should publish a notice warning that the entire de Beaune transaction was void. Secondly, a banker – Stuart suggested Rothschild – should discreetly buy up the bonds for a small percentage of their face value. This meant publicly repudiating the bonds while privately offering to buy them up from both fraudsters and genuine investors. At least one of George's officials from the old days advised caution before abandoning received wisdom and the matter lapsed for several years. However in January 1827 *The Times* carried a letter from the French press by a Chevalier d'Auriol stating that he, his sisters and others with whom he had made contact held bonds worth nearly half the amount of the loan. They intended to meet to determine how to obtain reimbursement, and they invited other investors to make themselves known.

Why it became necessary to put matters right a year later is unknown. Knighton disclosed only that if he were successful in his mission it would 'give a stability and security to [George's] *private affairs* and public character not to be questioned'. By 23 February 1828 Knighton was in Paris with plans to travel to Rotterdam, and deeply unhappy. Although his journal described sightseeing at St Cloud and Versailles, on 29 February he wrote to Dorothea from Paris that he was 'quite worn out with care and anxiety'. Tired and provoked, he claimed that he had 'never had any peace or comfort, and never expected any'. By aligning himself with Canning, Knighton had alienated both the Whigs and the remaining Tories. With Canning dead, Knighton had no one to defend him. On 19 February, a day after Duncombe's speech, a London publisher had issued a cartoon depicting Knighton as a gaunt, masked figure, grinding the crown and sceptre like a mortar and pestle to further his ambitions but losing influence as a winged Rothschild alighted with bags of gold to claim the title of 'de Incorporeal'. On 3 March *The Times* carried a letter from 'B.' – almost certainly Henry Brougham – asking whether the 'Invisible' had been McMahon's sole executor, commenting on McMahon's long service as private secretary at Carlton House, and ending with a Latin quotation from *Hamlet* which he translated as 'it means mischief'. When McMahon died in 1817 *The Times* had reported details of his will and named one of his half-brothers as his executor. However in 1828 *The Times*' editor answered B.'s question by stating that Knighton had been McMahon's sole executor.

On 8 March Knighton, still in Paris, informed Leveson-Gower that by means of his 'secret agency' and after 'no common Industry & management' he had discovered who held the notarial copy of the 'fraudulent Bond', although the figure he gave for the sum involved is not confirmed by other sources. However the de Beaune affair occupied only part of Knighton's thoughts. He interpreted Duncombe's speech as an attack on George, and in a rare lapse of logic and protocol he indulged in an epistolary rant, explaining to Leveson-Gower that he intended to mention the '*vile Slanderer* of his Majesty's most sacred name' in all letters that might be kept as records. Knighton returned to England a few days later and on 2 April Arthur Wellesley, now Prime Minister but still one of the new men, advised George that as the fraud had occurred forty years ago, and the people who could have proved George's innocence were dead, George had best shoulder the consequences of the fraud perpetrated in his name and buy up all the bonds. The matter must not go to court. Knighton returned to Paris. He now felt compromised by the people with whom he had to deal, both at home and abroad. Writing to Dorothea from Paris he concluded that the less collision one had with 'the lumps of clay of this life', the better. The Christian religion would, he railed, be possible if one 'could live alone at the back of a mountain' from birth. Two days later he wrote that an honest mind shrank from 'the crooked ways necessary to be pursued for the purpose of detecting fraud and villany' [sic]. Meanwhile work was accumulating in England. Writing from his temporary suite at St James's Palace, George hoped that Knighton could return immediately as work at both Windsor and Buckingham House had ceased. Knighton was back in May when he sat on the Bench as an expert adviser during a libel case between two artists. However the de Beaune affair was not yet settled.

On 23 May Harrison prepared a warrant authorising Knighton to buy up the bonds at five per cent of their face value. Knighton accompanied George to Windsor on 31 May and, while George was at Ascot, made his final recorded trip of the de Beaune affair. With him was Dora, and in consequence the journey was more leisurely, with the leg to Dover broken by an overnight stop. On arrival at Paris Knighton first visited the ambassador but afterwards he went sightseeing with Dora. They also took several meals at Very's, one of the innovative, attractive public rooms called restaurants where customers sat at small tables with companions of their choice, dined when they wished and chose food to suit their palates and their incomes. However it was not Knighton's frequent appearances in Paris in the company of his eldest daughter that attracted attention. Aspinall's *Letters* contain an account of Knighton's movements between April and June 1828 written by an agent. Who employed the agent, or how his report got into the royal papers, is unknown, but he described the parallel life of Knighton the proud father.

The agent's contact was the editor of a Whig publication, and son of a smuggler and a brothel keeper. The contact's sources were men at Dover and Boulogne who were allegedly Knighton's agents, and an Irishman who owed the contact a favour. The Irishman's brother taught in Paris, where his pupils included the adolescent son of a Government minister, and in return for a retainer the Irishman's brother would sell whatever political information he could discover. The contact reported that in Dover Knighton had been unable to conceal his identity, and that large boxes that arrived for him from Paris attracted much speculation. Once in Paris, however, Knighton had avoided places where people were on the lookout for him. The contact reported that Knighton's visits to France were 'related to some money transactions and other business of the King's when he was Prince of Wales'. A few cryptic lines, more damaging than the truth would have been, appeared in the press in mid-June 1828.

Knighton had returned by mid-July, when he received an uncharacteristically hostile letter from Richard Wellesley. During Robinson's tenure as Prime Minister Richard had come to London from Ireland, expecting that he would be invited to join the Government, and he remained in London with the same expectation when his brother, Arthur Wellesley, was appointed after Robinson's resignation. On 21 July, after waiting in vain for more than six months, Richard wrote to ask Knighton's assistance in getting his personal physician appointed serjeant-surgeon, a post that entailed accompanying George should he go into battle. However, describing himself as 'wholly out of power, insulted, and exiled', Richard wrote that he expected little from those who owed 'their very existence to his former kindness and indulgence'. He was not to know that a week earlier George had ordered Knighton to expedite the appointment of Astley Cooper. By late August 1828 Knighton was on the Continent again. The purpose of his journey is unclear but it probably involved meeting the Duke of Cumberland whose fanatic anti-Catholicism was becoming an embarrassment to Arthur Wellesley.

On his return Knighton replied to queries about George's health from the Duke of Clarence, who was now next in line to the throne, and the Duke of Cumberland wrote from the Continent asking to hear from Knighton as often as possible. Knighton did not forget his family and corresponded with William, now at Oxford, about life, literature and art, but he ended his letter of 7 November by describing himself as 'under the pressure of business and a thousand cares'. In early December the Court moved to Windsor Castle, its restoration complete, and Knighton then spent Christmas at Blendworth. During this time he again became ill, but on 2 February 1829, only recently recovered, he reluctantly left London for Berlin, protected against severe weather on the Continent by 'muffetees' – woolly scarves – sent up to town from Blendworth. Knighton's official task was to deliver 40,000 crowns from George to the Duke of Cumberland to repay a dowry owed to the family of the late king of Prussia, whose daughter had married the late Duke of York. Unofficially Knighton was to dissuade Cumberland from coming to England, where legislation for Roman Catholic emancipation was to be debated in Parliament.

Knighton reached Berlin on 15 February to find that Cumberland had left for England the previous week. Nevertheless Knighton was detained in Berlin where Cumberland's son, Prince George, had fallen seriously ill. Knighton urged bleeding from the arm, and George's tutor later recalled him pacing his apartments during the child's illness. Once the child began to recover Knighton returned to a changing Britain where the Roman Catholic Relief Act received Royal Assent on 10 April. Routine work continued. In May Walter Scott sent Knighton a new edition of the Waverley novels to present to George, who had a new family project. He was under the impression that Prince George, the Duke of Cumberland's son and heir to the throne of Hanover, could not receive his education in Britain. George therefore wanted George William, the Duke of Cambridge's son, to do so, but he was ambivalent as to whether he also wished the Duke and Duchess of Cambridge to leave Hanover and take up residence in England. Arthur Wellesley was against forcing Cambridge to resign as viceroy of Hanover, and on 20 June wrote urgently to Knighton proposing to call on him at Hanover Square on the night of Monday, 22 June. Monday was Dora's wedding day. Knighton saw her marry at eight o'clock in the morning, wept bitterly, and at one o'clock left for London with William. The next day, Tuesday, 23 June he made a pre-arranged visit to Windsor, then returned to town and that night met Arthur Wellesley and the Lord Chancellor. On Wednesday 'we' – Knighton, William and perhaps one other friend or relation – left Hanover Square at half past three in the morning and arrived at Calais the same day. It would be Knighton's last foreign journey of George's reign.

Chapter 8
1829–1830: The Final Year at Court

By the summer of 1829 George was nearly sixty-seven and Knighton was approaching his mid-fifties. Both were in poor health. George could barely see and had long been trapped in a cycle of weight gain that made him self-conscious about taking exercise, put strain on his heart and exacerbated joint pains. He also suffered severe bladder pains for which he took laudanum. Knighton's ill health was caused by worry, lack of sleep and unpredictable journeys undertaken in all weathers. By now every cold, infection and emotional stress incapacitated him.

George, who had given Dora a silver-gilt breakfast service as a wedding gift, regarded his officials' offspring as his extended family, and he was perhaps mellowed by her marriage to Seymour's son. As a result Knighton's journey of June and July 1829 was a royal mission extended into what George described as a 'matter of pleasure'. With Knighton was William, then eighteen. They travelled first to the German States via Paris and Antwerp where Knighton succumbed to his only outburst of the trip – on seeing how well a man could live in Antwerp on two hundred pounds a year he fumed to Dorothea that it was 'a waste of life and money' to live in England.

Knighton's mission was to discuss with the Duke and Duchess of Cambridge George's wish that their son be educated in England. On the way to Hanover he encountered them travelling with George's sister Elizabeth, the dowager landgravine of Hesse-Homburg, who had been widowed in April. He arranged to meet them the next day when, after braving the Duchess's tears, Knighton ascertained the feelings and finances of the recently bereaved Elizabeth, and especially what commitment she had made with Rothschild towards repaying a loan incurred by her late husband.

Knighton then travelled to Berlin, arriving on 17 July, where a letter from George was waiting. Loath though George was to curtail Knighton's trip, he needed him back at Court. Knighton replied that he would entirely put aside many of his plans and proceed at once to England via Paris. He and William then visited Luther's house at Wittemberg, heard the life story of the consul-general of Prussia at Leipzig, went sightseeing and picture-buying in Dresden and on 25 July, when his journal ended, he was still in the German States. Had George not been King of England both men would have recognised that their working relationship was reaching the end of its natural lifespan. However George was too ill, old and tired to replace Knighton, who could not in all decency desert the dying man whose dependency he had encouraged.

Knighton remained the first point of contact for those who had business with George. In mid-September 1829 he sent a line to a theatre proprietor who had understood that George disliked his box at Covent Garden, asking him not to trouble himself about an alternative for the time being. On 14 November John Ponsonby wrote to Knighton from Paris to say that he had just learnt of a new attempt by Harriette Wilson to blackmail him and that only deference to Elizabeth Conyngham's wishes prevented him from prosecuting Wilson. Frances Wilson describes Knighton's advice, which was once again to ignore Harriette. However relationships at Court were changing. George had already excluded from his circle Charles Sumner, whose rise in royal favour had almost brought down the Government nearly a decade earlier but who had alienated himself by supporting Roman Catholic emancipation. Knighton too was being eased from intimacy. On the same day that Ponsonby put pen to paper to write to Knighton, Arthur Wellesley sent a gossipy letter to Harriett Arbuthnot saying that Knighton and George had quarrelled at Windsor, that Knighton had been ordered to London in disgrace, that his career at Court was over and that it would be 'impossible to make use of him again as an Instrument'.

Knighton was now occupied by family concerns as Dora was pregnant with her first child, but Wellington was mistaken in believing that he had lost all favour at Court. Shortly before midnight on Boxing Day 1829, George wrote that Knighton was to come to Windsor by 29 December at the latest. If asked, he was to say that it was Duchy business. What the urgent business was, neither George nor Knighton committed to paper. Meanwhile on 28 December the Home Secretary sought Knighton's advice as to whether Manchester might be given a set of casts of the Elgin marbles.

Severely depressed, in January 1830 Knighton wrote to Dora that he had been 'a sad invalid' for the past ten or twelve days and that he would begin to wean his thoughts from life and prepare himself for 'that final resting-place that must soon come'. Dorothea described his mood as a 'melancholy tone of mind, induced by bodily ailment' that was fast creeping on him. Misfortunes that befell his friends exacerbated his depression. On 7 January 1830 Thomas Lawrence, who painted Knighton's portrait in 1822 and under whom William was said to have studied, died unexpectedly. At Lawrence's home were more than thirty pictures that George had commissioned for the Waterloo Gallery at Windsor Castle, and Knighton personally supervised their removal. Among Lawrence's unfinished works was a portrait of Dorothea which Knighton became anxious to retrieve. Robert Gooch and James Northcote were both ill. In late January Northcote entrusted his memoirs to Knighton for editing and publication but expressed doubts as to whether Knighton would have time to finish the task and lectured Knighton on the value of time. Meanwhile Knighton fretted over two landscapes by Dorothea, now in Northcote's possession, which Northcote, then in his eighties and one of the few people who could manipulate Knighton, appeared to be holding as ransom. Knighton remained ill. Unconvinced by reassurance from Henry Halford, one of George's senior physicians, that his heart was safe, Knighton once again broached with Dorothea the possibility of leaving Court. He tempered loyalty with prudence, and on falling ill he declined to attend at Windsor until he was well enough to travel. He arranged royal business so that he could be in town with William, writing afterwards to Dorothea, 'I love him so much, that whenever he goes to Oxford, I am always low.'

By 1830 Knighton was an ill, unhappy man, yet he was far from being the dogsbody suggested by the *Memoirs* and official correspondence. Aspinall's *Letters* include portions of Knighton's diary for February 1830 in which he recorded his exclusion from royal intimacy with detached amusement, speculating that George tolerated him only as a buffer against Elizabeth Conyngham. He attributed George's poor health to drink and conjectured that the King's heart was enlarged, 'much loaded with fat' and that death would be sudden. George believed that *The Times*, which had criticised him for not paying the debts of his late brother, the Duke of York, was controlled by Arthur Wellesley. Despite Wellesley's rebuke of 1827, Knighton dismissed the accusation as a lie.

Knighton nevertheless harboured his own suspicions about Arthur Wellesley who, he had previously observed, lacked interest in art. There was, Knighton believed, 'much to admire in him, but a good deal to wish different'. Writing to Harriett Arbuthnot six years earlier, Arthur Wellesley had claimed that there was no good reason to make 'the Barber' a peer or admit him to the Privy Council. Knighton now shrewdly remarked that Arthur Wellesley had 'no knowledge or power of judging that a man should be rewarded for civil service'. In addition Wellesley blamed the state of the nation on everyone wishing to acquire capital – in other words, Knighton observed, on people who wished to save. With Dora's confinement approaching, Knighton wrote to Dorothea, 'I only exist in the contemplation of my dear children.'

By late January Knighton was organising 9 Hanover Square in readiness for the birth of his first grandchild. Writing to Dora on 29 January he assumed that Michael would take the opportunity to 'ramble about with John, and look at good pictures'. Knighton's own movements, recorded in his original diary for 1 to 21 February 1830, reveal a surprising amount of time devoted to private business. He travelled repeatedly between Windsor and London, held meetings with Arthur Wellesley, attended to Duchy business and was ready to travel to Dusseldorf if necessary. However he also conversed at length with Northcote, bought paintings, viewed drawings from George's collection and praised da Vinci's knowledge of anatomy and physiology, and visited Blendworth, where he noted the progress of building and planting, played host to his in-laws and attended church. In addition between 2 and 4 February he paid daily visits to Gooch, who was dying. On 2 February Knighton described Gooch as wasted in body but mentally unimpaired. On 3 February Gooch was irritable, talking of life and death in the same breath, but still able to recommend a list of books for William that Knighton considered valuable enough to note. However Knighton's visit of 4 February distressed them both. Nearly four years earlier, when Gooch became too ill to practise medicine, Knighton had obtained for him the post of librarian at Carlton House. Under the stress of illness Gooch forgot this kindness. After the visit Knighton wrote in his diary, 'I must not go again – because there was nothing but abraidings that I would not get a place for him.' In response Knighton had neither remonstrated nor offered a patronising white lie of acquiescence, but simply asked Gooch how much the librarianship was worth. In the privacy of his diary Knighton commented with regret but not reproach that what Gooch lacked was Christian resignation. When Gooch died two weeks later Knighton visited his widow, met the executor and undertaker and arranged the funeral.

Nevertheless Knighton's original diary also portrays the calm, cheerful atmosphere that he sought for his daughter's confinement. Expecting that Dora would give birth in March, on 3 February he sought George's permission to go to Blendworth to see her. After a brief visit to Blendworth he left for town, but returned at the civilised hour of half past nine on the morning of Saturday, 13 February, having slept overnight at Godalming. He then spent three quiet days at home before bringing Dora to town on Wednesday, 17 February, accompanied by Sally Luscombe who had been staying at Blendworth. At Godalming they stopped and dined on boiled leg of mutton – no lowering regimen for Knighton's daughter. On 20 February Knighton went to Windsor, returning to Hanover Square to find that Dorothea had arrived with a letter from William.

Knighton's last surviving original diary entry, for 21 February, recorded a conversation with Arthur Wellesley and a visit to Northcote. The first reference to his grandchild, named Dorothea after her mother and grandmothers, comes from her baptism at Blendworth on 13 March 1830.

Her new life cheered and invigorated Knighton, and in late April he wrote to Dorothea from Windsor,

> I anticipate much happiness from our beloved Dora's return, with her darling little daughter, to Blendworth. May God make us thankful for this mercy! – it excites all one's thankfulness. . . . What a marvellous thing is time to look forward! but still more marvellous to look back.

For once Knighton viewed his life's progress and was pleased, but he was unable to join his family. The same letter revealed that he now slept in an adjacent room to George, who wanted him always near. Knighton foresaw that if George's latest bout of illness did not abate quickly its course would be cruel.

Knighton believed that his duty now was to promote George's comfort and peace of mind, and he foresaw that in consequence he would be attacked in public. Previously, when Knighton had used his initiative to act in George's interests – for example, by ending secret diplomacy with foreign powers, reducing George's personal expenditure and getting official documents signed – his actions had also been in the interest of the country. Now Knighton sought to save George from having to cope with the constitutional implications of a monarch's impending death. However George, despite his pain, had days when he felt cheerful and able to enjoy himself. He did not perceive himself as a man of declining powers. Anxious to conceal his difficulties, he struggled to sign documents by hand rather than explain to Parliament why he needed an official stamp.

George became sceptical about the advice of his usual medical attendants and sent for James Wardrop who had accompanied him to Scotland in 1822. Wardrop had been appointed a surgeon-in-ordinary in 1828 but was not one of George's regular medical attendants. However he treated at least one of his horses, and only the best was good enough for George's stud. On 25 April 1830 Wardrop attended George at Windsor, and the interview was described in Thomas Pettigrew's *Medical Portrait Gallery*, published ten years later. Wardrop was alone with George, who asked about recovery. Wardrop's prognosis was that George was seriously ill but that his death was not inevitably imminent. After forty minutes Knighton entered the room and Wardrop left. George reported

1829–1830: The Final Year at Court

Wardrop's opinion to Knighton, who asked Wardrop to write up his suggested treatment in a letter that Knighton would give to Henry Halford, the most senior physician in attendance at Windsor. Wardrop complied and awaited a summons that never came, while learning that George frequently asked why Wardrop did not visit him. According to Pettigrew, Knighton failed to hand over the letter. Pettigrew also claimed that on the day Knighton died Dorothea wrote to Wardrop, saying that only 'hurry and anxiety of mind' had caused the omission, and that towards the end of his life Knighton had wished that he could call Wardrop to his bedside to clear up the misunderstanding. Whatever the truth, Wardrop believed that he had been ignored and that George was the worse for it.

Meanwhile Knighton was still George's man of business. The dying monarch remained a source of donations, and Clarence and Cumberland received money for their charitable causes. Scott, who had suffered a stroke, asked whether he might receive a pension if he retired from his post as Clerk of Session. George's siblings enquired about their brother's health, with Cambridge and the dowager landgravine Elizabeth especially anxious as to whether they should remain abroad or travel to Windsor. On 7 May Bloomfield wrote to Knighton about his distress on learning of George's condition. He also reported that he had written to 'Lord L****' to settle a 'hateful affair' which had caused trouble for Knighton, but did not name it. Outside the sick room the country was gearing up to electoral reform and openness. It was no longer acceptable for a street and a few fields in Bere Alston to have two Members of Parliament. The same sentiments held it increasingly less acceptable for officials to hold sinecures and be paid for jobs they did not do in order to compensate them for jobs that they should not be doing. On 25 May Knighton told Dorothea that he had a box into which he threw, unread, the 'filth' with which he was favoured. His duties for the dying George were, he wrote, enough to destroy his constitution. His life was miserable and wretched and he wished it were over. Two days later, still unwell but comforted by a reply from Dorothea, Knighton reported that George was 'particularly affectionate' to him. George's health was gradually breaking down but he had a strong constitution and his remaining lifespan could not be calculated.

Sir William Knighton

Wardrop had contacts in the medical press, and on 12 June *The Times* published reports from the *Lancet* and the *London Medical Gazette* accusing all George's medical attendants of misconduct. The cautious bulletins issued by Henry Halford and Matthew Tierney, who had warned of George's precipitous health in 1822, were said to be deliberately misleading. Knighton was the 'enchanter' and 'magician' under whose 'invisible' influence Tierney signed bulletins without seeing George. The accusation against Tierney was later retracted. George died on 26 June.

In the following months Knighton continued to be the listening ear into which those with business with George poured their troubles. George was not yet buried when the architect John Nash, required to produce accounts, wrote to Knighton saying that his spirit was quite broken and that he was incapable of business. The dowager landgravine Elizabeth described to Knighton her grief and sprained knee and thanked him for his many kindnesses. Historians depict Knighton and Arthur Wellesley sorting through George's possessions as part of their executors' duties and finding bundles of ancient love letters, locks of women's hair and sexually explicit art that they considered best burnt. On learning of George's death Elizabeth Conyngham was alleged to have commenced a lengthy packing session and confrontations over jewels were rumoured. However these incidents had more to do with George than with Knighton, who was eager to let go of his brief but all-consuming second career. As George was interred his chief household officers broke their staves of office and placed them on his coffin. Their obligation was to the monarch, not to the monarchy. Knighton had no stave to break, but George's death none the less released him from a post that James Northcote described as 'not so soft a seat as some people might imagine'. Northcote summed up Knighton's success by saying that George was lazy and Knighton made everything easy for him. In early July 1830 Knighton, who a few weeks earlier had wished himself dead, rejoiced that he had 'a home and sincerity and affection to fly to' and hoped that God would grant him ten years in which to enjoy them. Without a moment's nostalgia he planned to dispose of 9 Hanover Square, the royal physician's home that he had acquired as an ambitious newcomer more than twenty years earlier, and at the end of September he sold the remainder of the lease to Charles Locock, a protégé of Robert Gooch and former pupil of Benjamin Brodie. At thirty-one, Locock was perhaps only a year older than Knighton had been when he first moved to No 9.

On 14 July, his career as a courtier at an end and no longer a source of patronage with the ear of the monarch, Knighton received a letter from Walter Scott. In the past Scott had used every contact with Knighton to press for favours, but now there were no more favours to be had, Scott proved himself no fair-weather friend and discreetly pledged his influence on Knighton's behalf. Scott elegantly refuted the allegations against Knighton but, knowing the distress they caused, gave no hint that he knew of them. He wrote that 'friends in the North' knew that Knighton had fulfilled his royal duties at the cost of his health. Scott understood that it might be a relief to leave Court, but was sad that the change had been brought about by the loss of Knighton's 'friend and benefactor'. Seldom had a subject shown his sovereign 'such disinterested and attached zeal'. Knighton's services to George were 'universally acknowledged' and he possessed 'the approbation of the world'. Finally, Scott asked for something. When Knighton had time, would he spare Scott a line to tell him how he was? It would, Scott wrote, be highly valued.

Chapter 9

Colleague, Friend and Fellow Traveller

Walter Scott reassured Knighton without referring to the reasons that necessitated reassurance. That was how gentlemen communicated with each other, and it was a technique that Knighton had had to learn. By the time he became a courtier he had replaced unnecessary classical allusions with politeness, an eighteenth-century concept that meant establishing mutually advantageous contacts across a limited range of social divides by avoiding unnecessary disagreement. He established civil working relationships regardless of mutual antipathy, while his tact and general demeanour inspired confidences. Knighton cherished his privacy but he was neither antisocial nor unsocial. The *Memoirs* recorded his dislike of travelling alone, and when he lacked a companion he extracted life stories from complete strangers. His empathy worked as effectively on a clergyman's cook as on a widowed princess and, schooled by many years of writing case notes, he remembered, recorded and analysed what had been confided.

The *Memoirs* let slip that when Knighton was unwell he could be embarrassingly pompous, but overall they portray an earnest youth, a hardworking family man and a loyal, able but maligned royal servant. He was motivated by what he believed to be his father's shameful behaviour and the death of his own first-born son in 1802. Contemporaries who included Knighton in their own memoirs described his sensitivity to criticism, his willingness to help his friends and his ultimate unhappiness in royal service, while unpublished letters portray a man who could harbour resentment but who always had time for his friends. He was a decent man who fretted over what others thought of him, stood high in his own estimation, and craved both a stable home and worldly recognition. He believed in respectability, propriety and adherence to social norms yet enjoyed the company of witty, educated men whose private lives reflected different values. Tiredness and ill health brought out the worst in him. A friend in need received pertinent advice and practical help.

Colleague, Friend and Fellow Traveller

Knighton's friendships were formed within a limited social circle. Of the chalk-and-cheese Wellesley brothers, neither Arthur, with whom he dined and conducted business but for whom he had limited respect, nor Richard, whose wit and erudition he admired, became friends. Also outside the circle was Knighton's secretary, Thomas Marrable, who had shown the same discretion as Knighton in the McMahon affair but who did not become a royal confidant. On one occasion Knighton was glad to have Marrable as a companion rather than travel alone but he did not write of him as an intimate. Instead Knighton's friends were gentlemen professionals whom he met during his two careers, and several friendships were strengthened by links with the Seymours and Hawkers.

The medical establishment in Plymouth had been jealous of Knighton's early success and the Royal College of Physicians in London had tried to exclude him, yet it was Knighton's first career, rather than his second, that provided three of the four friends who attended his funeral. One was Benjamin Brodie, who was appointed George's surgeon in 1828. He was at Windsor Castle when George died but escaped press censure. Brodie wrote that in 1815 he performed an autopsy on one of Knighton's patients at the request of dissatisfied relatives and entirely vindicated Knighton's treatment. Knighton never referred to the incident, but two or three years later he became what Brodie described as one of Brodie's 'warmest and kindest friends'. A biography of Brodie contained a letter from Knighton to Brodie written in retirement. Knighton doubted whether they would meet often but wanted Brodie to know that he would always remember with pleasure the time they spent together.

Like Knighton, Brodie had arrived in London only to find that he could not practise as a physician without a degree, but whereas Knighton was determined to pursue physic, Brodie remained a surgeon. All they had in common were large incomes from fees and positions in George's household. Brodie had been educated to a high standard by his father and was related to leading members of the medical establishment. Six or seven years younger than Knighton, he obtained a hospital appointment while

Knighton was still in Edinburgh, was elected to the Royal Society soon after Knighton's return from the Peninsula, and became a professor of the Royal College of Surgeons while Knighton was supplanting Bloomfield. Brodie considered that apprenticeship to an apothecary, which was the basis of Knighton's knowledge, was an 'absurd system' and, in painful contrast with Knighton's derivative essay on putrid fever, regularly published medical articles based on original observations. He moved in higher social circles than did Knighton and during their lifetimes was enshrined in stone in the Temple of Worthies at the home of his Whig relative, Sir George Staunton of Leigh Park, only a few miles from Blendworth. Surviving the stigma attached to George's Court, Brodie held the honorary post of serjeant-surgeon under William IV and Queen Victoria and he used his biography to distance himself from their forebear's dearest friend. Conceding that Knighton had much practical knowledge, he wrote that Knighton lacked scientific attainments and had pursued medicine only to earn a living. Brodie implied that Dorothea was Knighton's superior in morals, intellect and accomplishments. According to Brodie, although Knighton had accepted the post of Keeper of the Privy Purse against her advice, she subsequently pointed out that he could not resign with honour while George was still dependent on him. Brodie acknowledged Knighton's insight into men's characters and the ways of the world, but dismissed it as compensation for an imperfect education that had left Knighton 'deficient' in some of the qualities necessary for general society. In other words, Knighton had had the good fortune to be born with a good brain, but he could never be Brodie's equal.

The second mourner was Stephen Hammick, with whom Knighton had worked at the Royal Naval Hospital at Plymouth and whom he had described as 'born with the knife in his hand'. Hammick had trained on the job at the Royal and did not hold a degree. In August 1799 Hammick and Knighton had both resigned, Knighton to pursue full-time private practice in Plymouth, Hammick to walk the wards at St George's Hospital, London, as Knighton had done at St Thomas's. After a few months Hammick returned to the Royal where he stayed for nearly thirty years. He belonged to the scientific medical community by virtue of his skill and his post at a prestigious hospital, and in 1806, when Knighton was contemplating the potato diet, Hammick was appointed surgeon-extraordinary to George. By the time of Knighton's funeral Hammick had published extensively and had a thriving private practice.

The third mourner was William Chambers who, with Martin Tupper, attended Knighton's final illness. Chambers was a respected physician but his practice had been slow to become successful. By the time of Knighton's final illness Chambers was suffering the effects of a poisoned wound sustained during a post mortem for which he had been treated by Brodie. However two weeks after Knighton's death he received the first of several royal appointments. Martin Tupper was joined to the Knightons by friendship. Tupper's son had been William's contemporary at both Charterhouse and Christ Church and later named a son William Knighton Tupper.

Of the group of five from Edinburgh, only Robert Gooch and Henry Southey survived to witness Knighton's change of profession. Both benefited. Southey was appointed physician-in-ordinary when Knighton resigned in 1823, and when Gooch became too ill to practise Knighton obtained for him the post of librarian at Carlton House. Gooch became a family friend. He advised the newly-married Dora, prescribed for Dorothea, and was the Knightons' only known guest at Sherwood Lodge. Brodie and Chambers, who shared similar liberal politics, and the apolitical, self-effacing but brilliant Hammick were welcome guests at Holland House, the Whig salon named after the title of the Fox family whose London home it was. Knighton encountered the Holland House family on official business. As he explained to Canning, to avoid being compromised he declined invitations to dine.

As a London physician Knighton chose not to socialise so as to be available for work. However in the Peninsula he relished being part of Richard Wellesley's suite and returned to England having made a lifelong friend. This was not the astute, witty but risqué Benjamin Sydenham whom Knighton had considered a benefit to the party, but Samuel Ford Whittingham, an army officer who was convalescing at Richard Wellesley's Seville residence and who knew one of Dorothea's brothers. Whittingham found a horse sufficiently small to entice Knighton to put his foot in the stirrup, and they rode together every day at five o'clock in the cool of the morning. The *Memoirs* recorded Knighton's pleasure at their daily rides, and Whittingham's own memoir, published thirty years later, generously concurred. Although Whittingham became a career soldier he had been educated for the law and had worked for his family's merchant firm. His unusual background perhaps equipped him to see the best in Knighton, who was among the circle of friends who used the contraction 'Samford'. Whittingham was in England in October 1836. It was he who informed William IV's secretary of Knighton's imminent death, and after Knighton's death it was Whittingham to whom Arthur Wellesley wrote in order to contact William.

From his years as a courtier Knighton gained the friendship of the cultured, elegant Charles Sumner, former tutor to Elizabeth Conyngham's sons, later George's chaplain and librarian and finally Bishop of Winchester. After supporting Roman Catholic emancipation Sumner lost George's favour, but by then the friendship between Knighton and Sumner was established. In June 1829 Sumner married Dora to Michael, and two years later, when Sumner suffered a life-threatening fever, Knighton hurried to his bedside to take charge of the sickroom.

Other friendships grew from shared secrets and responsibilities. Although Knighton's foreign journeys attracted speculation, in certain circles their details were common knowledge. As Keeper of the Privy Purse and in his posts in the Duchies of Cornwall and Lancaster, Knighton arranged secret royal financial transactions with senior but unassuming officials whom no one thought to accuse or question. George Harrison, Knighton's successor as auditor of the Duchy of Cornwall, attracted no censure when he quietly acquired the additional auditorship of Lancaster three years later. In the winter of 1823 Harrison was involved in the mortgage of George's Hanoverian income to Rothschilds, and in a letter to George he referred unambiguously to a fund of £5,000 'for secret and collateral services connected with your Majesty's service'. In the de Beaune crisis of 1828 it was Harrison who prepared the warrant authorising Knighton to buy back the £100 bonds, although spies who followed Knighton from London to Paris and back knew only of mysterious boxes. Also privy to royal secrets was Andrew Dickie, chief clerk and later a partner at Coutts. A travelling companion during Knighton's retirement, Dickie understood Knighton's vulnerability and on his deathbed took pains to vindicate Knighton's handling of George's finances.

The *Memoirs*, Wellington's correspondence and Aspinall's *Letters* all confirm that Knighton made the Privy Purse debt-free. However no one who praised Knighton's stewardship of George's finances explained how he achieved royal solvency. The records of the Duchies of Cornwall and Lancaster are the personal papers of the royal family, so they are not available to the public, but fortunately there is now detailed published information about Lancaster. During the twentieth century Sir Robert Somerville, a Duchy of Lancaster official whose posts included Keeper of the Records, wrote a history of the Duchy for his colleagues. His second volume, issued in 1970, includes the Knighton era, and two years later he wrote specifically about the Duchy's officers. The following account is based entirely on his work.

When Knighton joined the Duchy of Lancaster it occupied a new office only yards from the Duchy of Cornwall's rooms in Somerset House, where Knighton was auditor and then Receiver-General. The new premises were long wished for and became possible when some buildings from the old Savoy Hospital were demolished to create an approach to the new Waterloo Bridge. The purpose-built office reflected the Duchy's ideals, for though the Duchy guarded its private, non-governmental status, it was keen to improve its efficiency. The most senior Duchy post, that of Chancellor, was a political appointment in the gift of the monarch. The Receiver-General was appointed for life, sometimes at the monarch's suggestion, and other vacancies were filled by recommendation. Officers often held more than one post in both Cornwall and Lancaster and, as Lancaster also operated its own courts, many of its officers were lawyers. Robert Harper, who bridged the old and new reigns, attended Westminster School, was articled to the Duchy Solicitor, became Solicitor himself, and by Knighton's time was Deputy – that is, acting – Clerk to the Council. His successor was Frederick Danvers, a clerk from the Duchy of Cornwall. Harrison was a barrister. Nevertheless it was Knighton the farmer's son who in 1826 was made Receiver-General at Lancaster. In addition a new post of Vice-Chancellor was created especially for him to provide continuity during changes of Chancellor. As Vice-Chancellor Knighton was directly responsible to George and was specifically required to improve revenues and efficiency.

A deputy post usually meant performing the duties of the senior official, and Somerville notes that as Vice-Chancellor Knighton attended meetings of the Duchy Council even when the Chancellor was present. However Knighton also performed his own Receiver-General's duties, and he travelled to the north of England to inspect Duchy woods. When Knighton left Court after George's death, Needwood Forest provided an opportunity to stay with a friend, Lord Vernon of Sudbury Hall, and in a charming letter to Mary Frances Knighton explained that he and Lord Vernon would be travelling to London with a potato pasty apiece to avoid breaking their journey. Under Knighton the Duchy made unspectacular but effective changes. Local receivers were told to send their takings to London as soon as they received them instead of keeping them to pay expenses. Accounts were to show all sums received and expenses paid, not what was left after subtracting the latter from the former. Rent collection was reviewed. Accounts and trusts started to be held by the Duchy, not by named officers, and the Duchy asked the Ordnance Department, which was conducting surveys in order to publish maps, for tracings of surveys that included Duchy property.

Colleague, Friend and Fellow Traveller

As Vice-Chancellor Knighton was empowered to make certain appointments, and he did not shrink from exercising patronage in favour of people he trusted. His Deputy-Receiver at both Cornwall and Lancaster was his younger half-brother, John Tolle. Robert Harper lived for a further two decades after being pensioned off to make way for Frederick Danvers, whom Knighton knew from the Duchy of Cornwall, whom he appointed co-executor with Dorothea and William, and who subsequently helped Dorothea publish the *Memoirs*. Danvers' post came with residential accommodation at the new office, and Somerville believed that it was Knighton who authorised expenditure of nearly £900 on the Clerk of the Council's quarters to accommodate Danvers' growing family.

Not everything at Court was to be shunned. George was a patron of the arts, and as Privy Purse Knighton dealt with artists on George's behalf, becoming known as a connoisseur in his own right. Artists were fellow gentlemen professionals and he sought their friendship. Thomas Lawrence's correspondence at the Royal Academy portrays a difficult relationship, initially formal, but closer after Knighton sat for Lawrence in 1822. Knighton preferred amiable contact with Lawrence, offering a seat in his carriage, sending pills and recommending a dinner of basted chicken when Lawrence had a severe cold, and expressing amiable envy at the contents of Lawrence's home. Lawrence's notorious slowness at finishing commissions required all Knighton's tact. On one occasion Knighton suggested that a note expressing a Royal request had perhaps been mislaid and not reached Lawrence. On another he stressed that Lawrence 'must have the goodness, not to fail' to obey a command to attend Windsor to finish a portrait, and recommended a room with good light where Lawrence could work. A month later however Knighton was obliged to convey George's formal command that Lawrence was to finish the portrait without delay and send it to Carlton House. When dealing with his own commissions Knighton busied himself in every aspect, from sitting to framing. John Linnell is now best known for his landscapes and for his support for William Blake, but during the years when Knighton collected paintings, Linnell was a portrait painter, and in the late 1820s and early 1830s he painted several members of the family. Knighton dropped in on artists at their studios to be allowed privileged views of their works in progress and to discuss art and artists. He was especially close to David Wilkie, a successful Scottish artist whose genre paintings told stories of everyday life. At the time of Knighton's greatest influence Wilkie was established and successful, but when ill health and depression threatened Wilkie's career Knighton encouraged George to support him with purchases. Wilkie received more of the rarely-extended invitations to Blendworth than he was able to accept, and regarded Knighton as his best and irreplaceable friend and adviser.

Other friends welcome in Knighton's household were Thomas Stepney – eccentric, charming, studiously old-fashioned, and a favourite with Dora – and his wife Catherine, a former patient, sometime novelist and writers' hostess. In her letter of condolence to Dorothea on Knighton's death, Catherine wrote that Knighton had comforted and protected her in her misery and described him as 'considerate in emergency'. His sympathy took the form of effective action. In August 1827, between Canning's death and yet another foreign trip, Knighton received a letter regarding the widow of his late colleague, Christopher Pemberton, who had died in 1822 after much ill health. Knighton replied with a courteous, one-sentence reply and a draft for £100 to be forwarded to Mrs Pemberton.

A woman who suffered loss, as his mother had done, always tugged at his heartstrings. However although Knighton adored his mother, his idealised woman was not a young widow with two small children who ran a large farm and sold butter and eggs at Plymouth market. Instead she was wise but demure, and he formed platonic but devoted relationships that must have caused Dorothea private unease. Among the people to whom Geach introduced Knighton were the Treby family. Paul Treby was Member of Parliament for Plympton. His wife, Letitia, was about fifteen years older than Knighton. Knighton felt able to confide in her, and he could confide to her in writing, which was perhaps not possible with Dorothy. In letters to Letitia Treby, preserved for more than thirty years and entrusted to Dorothea for inclusion in the *Memoirs*, Knighton described the traumas in his life –

the secrecy about his background, the jealously and gossip he suffered in Plymouth and the death of his first-born son. As a young man Knighton had what can only be termed as a crush on Letitia Treby. On one occasion he wrote to her on a large folio sheet edged with gold leaf, and responded to her surprise by explaining that she deserved a decoration of gold and that he needed a large sheet of paper to express the breadth of his pleasure in writing to her. The young Mrs Knighton must have been relieved that Letitia Treby did not, as Knighton wished, live next door. Though easy to ridicule, the friendship between Knighton and Letitia was sincere, and it deepened to shared grief when each lost a son.

In his fifties Knighton was still forming chaste but intense friendships with women. The *Memoirs* contains a letter from Knighton dated about 1826 to an unnamed friend who had written to him about religious belief. We do not know whether Knighton had been asked a specific question or whether he had discerned an unstated worry in his friend's letter, but he replied by explaining his beliefs on life after death, citing the Scriptures in support and, with great propriety yet unmistakable meaning, extending his hypothesis to relationships between husbands and wives in heaven. Knighton believed that in heaven the dead were resurrected in a bodily form of God's choosing, never to die again. Because they did not die they no longer needed to procreate, and as a result they ceased to experience sexual attraction. Marriages ended by death on earth were not resumed in heaven, although the love that men and women had felt for each other in life survived in a purified form that transcended earthly considerations. Knighton's interpretation meant that widows and widowers should not be deterred from remarriage by fear of painful encounters in afterlife, and was of more than academic interest to his correspondent. Other sources identify her as Anne Grey, one of Reverend Sir Samuel's daughters, a widow in her twenties, little more than half Knighton's age, and perhaps a year younger than Dorothy had been when Knighton's father died. Grey had been renting The Grove, about a mile from Blendworth Cottage and within sight of Blendworth House, and in the autumn of 1827, to the delight of her friends, she became engaged.

Sir William Knighton

The correspondence at West Sussex Record Office that reveals the existence of Knighton's property in Nice includes letters of congratulation to Grey from Dora, also newly engaged, from William and from Dorothea – Dorothea teased that Grey was probably not quite so occupied as were *some* ladies on similar occasions. Other congratulations were equally cheerful and sincere, with one older man trusting that she would not forget her '*old & humble* Servant'. Writing on 26 November 1827, Knighton at first took the same tone, and he offered to become one of Grey's trustees if she was not already covered by family arrangements. Towards the end of his letter however he strove to convey a more personal message. He noted his unsteady hand and continued, 'There is so much mixed up with it, – that it is so no easy matter to say, what one would wish.' Abandoning the attempt he ended, 'You have followed my advice. God bless you!' However he was unable to leave his thoughts unexpressed and added a postscript, paraphrasing Edmund Burke, the late-eighteenth-century philosopher and statesman. 'The Passions', Knighton explained, 'are of a complicated kind & branch out into a variety of forms agreeable to the variety of ends they are to serve in the great chain of Society!' He told Grey that everyone wanted to have someone to call on in time of need. The relationship was so close that he called it 'a substitute ... for ourselves'. He concluded,

> I *know* what living alone is, & although I am growing old, I know the difficulty of trimming one's thoughts to that insulated state. – You have done quite right in the decision you have taken, & I trust in God the happiest part of Your Life is yet to come. God bless you.

Anne Grey was too young to accept an insulated state, and passions of a complicated kind were nature's way of ensuring that she would have a companion and protector, and a substitute for herself. She no longer needed a confidant, and the following month Knighton sent her a cheerful, avuncular note, conveying universal approval of her future husband.

The romantic or sociable Knighton was known to only a few. Better known was his gratitude for past help. Henry Fox, Lord Holland, the final Chancellor of the Duchy of Lancaster under whom Knighton served, observed in his diary that Knighton was 'mindful of kindnesses', and the *Memoirs* bore him out. Knighton envisaged that Dorothea's 'little book' would prove 'comforting and consolatory' to those for whom it was intended, and the *Memoirs* named many people for no other reason than to record Knighton's fellow feeling or esteem. Lacroix, the British Consul at Nice, could read that Knighton had grieved to learn of the death of his daughter and remembered her as 'a pretty little girl'. The *Memoirs*' deferential references to Jane Metzler, governess to Knighton's children and grandchildren, told the world that the King's dearest friend respected her advice. Knighton practised condescension in the original sense of the word, meaning that he could extend courtesy to people of lower social standing without creating awkwardness. It was part of the bedside manner that he had been perfecting since his teens.

However Fox also observed that Knighton was 'not less resentful of injuries'. Northcote said that Knighton was afraid of being talked about or of 'making enemies through envy', and throughout his life Knighton fretted over untruths spread about him. Some of his contemporaries claimed that he had a foul temper and was obsessed with money, but this was gossip intended to discredit the Plymouth shop boy. A substantiated example of a churlish Knighton withholding co-operation comes from none other than his friend, Charles Sumner. Sumner's biography omitted the incident, and at the time Knighton was in dangerously poor health. However the Ward archive at the Centre for Buckinghamshire Studies contains an unpublished letter of December 1835 from Sumner, then Bishop of Winchester, to an unnamed correspondent who had sought Sumner's intervention to improve his poor relationship with Knighton. The correspondent was almost certainly the new Blendworth Rector, Edward Langton Ward. Sumner sympathised with his predicament, advising him to endeavour 'not to see any coldness' even when it was 'too apparent to be overlooked'. Sumner offered no justification for Knighton's behaviour, for it was to bridge divides such as that between rector and baronet that politeness had evolved. Knighton's feelings for the Blendworth that lay beyond the boundaries of his home were ambivalent. According to the *Memoirs* he readily gave medical advice to anyone who needed it, regardless of class, and as a result became 'much beloved'. Nevertheless Wilkie believed that it was unusual for Knighton to dine away from home at Blendworth. Moreover, as local historian John Merrell discovered, Knighton was buried not at the parish church of St Giles but in a spacious vault at the new cemetery at Kensall Green in London where, of all his relations, only John Tolle chose to join him.

The younger, healthier Knighton of a decade or so earlier was good company, and the compliment comes from a man with whom he had nothing in common. Nearly twenty years younger than Knighton, Sir Denis Le Marchant was educated at Eton and Cambridge, became a barrister, supported reform and became Henry Brougham's secretary. How Knighton and Le Marchant came to socialise is a mystery but, after describing Knighton as ambitious and scheming, Le Marchant added that he had 'refined tastes and winning manners' and was 'a very agreeable companion'. Le Marchant credited Knighton with being the originator and perpetuator of the old chestnut concerning George, Napoleon and Caroline:

'Sire – your greatest enemy is dead.'

'When did she die?'

A fragment of Knighton's diary for November 1830, reproduced in Aspinall's *Letters*, included an anecdote about McMahon's wife jumping from a window into a courtyard to avoid using the street and having to be revived by George with a large glass of sherry. The doting father and harassed royal servant was, when he chose to be, an accomplished raconteur.

On occasion courtly or convivial language lacked urgency, and when his friends' interests were at stake Knighton was blunt. In 1826 James Seymour, Seymour's second son, was appointed aide-de-camp to Samford Whittingham in India. Because of the slowness of communication by sea, Knighton wrongly believed that the first Whittingham would know of this was when James arrived. Providing James with a letter of introduction, Knighton stressed that George took great interest in the family of Seymour, the captain of his yacht – in other words, accepting James would do Whittingham's career no harm. Knighton's advice to Sumner was even more forthright – 'be so good as to get rid of your shirt-frill and trousers' he urged Sumner in June 1825 when Jenkinson finally abandoned his objections and acceded to George's wish that Sumner be made a bishop. Sumner became a bishop but his dress sense remained unchanged. Writing a hostile obituary of Sumner many years later, the Rector of Farlington near Portsmouth pointedly selected for praise Sumner's fashionable attire.

Benjamin Brodie wrote that to discuss a subject with Knighton was to conclude that he was in complete agreement. Aspinall's *Letters* include the example of Lewis Way, who ran an English church in Paris and whose life's mission was to convert the Jews to Christianity. In financial difficulty and on the basis of what he believed was a 'friendly overture' from Knighton, Way suggested that Knighton buy some of his land at Stansted, a few miles from Blendworth, or perhaps lend him £10,000. In private Knighton considered that Way was an extremist and that all extremes were ill judged. Friendships recorded elsewhere were equally illusory. Aspinall's *Letters* contain effusive thanks from Bloomfield to Knighton, yet Bloomfield's biography pointedly omitted the years 1817 to 1822 during which Knighton supplanted him. Similarly, in selecting correspondence for the *Memoirs* Dorothea failed to distinguish between civility and friendship, especially where George's siblings were concerned. Nevertheless her unlikely assertion that Knighton 'had for many years been on very friendly terms with Lord and Lady Brougham' was true. Among Alfred Morrison's *Autograph Letters* is one from Brougham saying how much 'M[rs] B.', who was in poor health, would appreciate a visit from Knighton, and Knighton and Brougham exchanged detailed, scholarly correspondence during the cholera outbreaks of the early 1830s.

Though Knighton had friends and sympathisers he confided completely in no one. Brodie was unaware that Knighton had arranged with George to retrieve papers from McMahon. As a consequence he believed what he acknowledged was the generally accepted rumour that Knighton had been McMahon's executor, and that in the course of his executor's duties found papers that were embarrassing to George and used them to his advantage. And if one of Knighton's few close friends believed the worst of him, what would his enemies surmise?

CHAPTER 10
MYTH, MISTAKE AND DISCREPANCY

Henry Fox described Knighton as 'a Man of business and sense and of a strange career' whose love of mystery probably made him pass for a much worse man than he really was. Fox was unaware of the extent to which Knighton had mystery forced upon him, but his verdict explains history's qualified approval of George's 'dear friend'. The most inconsequential details of Knighton's life are obscured by discrepancies, and the cumulative impression is that of a man whom no one really knew.

Because Knighton was mistaken about his family history he misled Dorothea, and as a result the *Memoirs* misrepresented his early life. Of his adult life, a few letters were wrongly dated or out of sequence, and on one occasion Knighton deliberately gave Dorothea a flawed account which she had no means of verifying. Otherwise most of her 'little book', especially the dates of Knighton's travels and meetings, can be corroborated by other sources. Its publication was allegedly awaited with a mixture of apprehension and relish but, as one reviewer observed, the 'good feeling' of Knighton's family prevented it from containing the information that people most wanted to read. Aspinall compared material in the *Memoirs* with originals in the Royal Archives and found that Dorothea edited the originals to preserve the confidentiality that Knighton had practised during his life, although one omission – the loss of 'not' from 'The King was not particularly glad to see me' – was a slip of the pen by a recently-bereaved widow. Unwisely, Dorothea included in the *Memoirs* an indifferent obituary of Knighton first published in the *Medical Gazette* and repeated in *The Times*. With this exception the *Memoirs* comprised her edited versions of his journals and correspondence linked by what Richard Grenville described as her own 'unpretending narrative', meaning that she limited her contribution to family and personal details with no comment on the events in which her husband was involved. This makes parts of the *Memoirs* incomprehensible to most modern readers – including this biographer – without background information.

Knighton's contemporaries produced highly readable anecdotes about him, but most had no intention of letting objectivity spoil a good yarn. With one exception they were Tories. Not all wrote for publication and in most cases edited editions of their writings were not published until the twentieth century. Harriett Arbuthnot's journal and Dorothea Lieven's letters, not intended for publication, recorded current Tory Ultra gossip about Knighton. Henry Hobhouse's diary, written for a wider readership but not published until the twentieth century, covered most of his years as an under-secretary of state in Jenkinson's Government and mixed diary entries with recollections. Hobhouse's editor, Arthur Aspinall, described Hobhouse as 'a Tory of the old-fashioned type'. Out of sympathy with Canning's support for Roman Catholic emancipation, Hobhouse was suspicious of the turncoat Knighton. Thomas Raikes is remembered as a club man and diarist but he was also a merchant; the raconteur Captain Gronow described him as the 'city dandy' whose jokes were 'stale' and who was the butt of his aristocratic companions. Raikes did not begin his journal until 1831, probably intending it for publication. It contained a high proportion of recollections. Charles Greville, a friend of Arthur Wellesley and manager of the Duke of York's stud, was for nearly forty years Clerk of the Privy Council, membership of which was denied Knighton. Greville was fascinated by diaries, edited Raikes's journal and kept one himself. He described his youthful entries as 'horrid trash' but believed that a diary was a place in which to revise one's beliefs with no obligation to be consistent. Greville did not write for publication but realised that publication was likely. The sole Whig was Thomas Creevey, a Member of Parliament for most of Knighton's working life, frequently impecunious but a welcome society house guest. Creevey's letters, preserved and transcribed by a stepdaughter for a history that he never got round to writing, were published in the twentieth century. Like Lieven and Arbuthnot, he recorded current events rather than recollections.

Sir William Knighton

Mischief-making, genuine mistakes and gossip have created sufficient material for an alternative biography of Knighton. Some of this can be exposed as fiction. The rest, however unlikely, can be neither proved nor disproved, an uncomfortable reminder of how little we know about him. According to Raikes, Knighton was born to parents of 'humble origin' who placed him with an apothecary in Tavistock. The year of his birth is uncertain. The *Memoirs* gave it as 1776 and according to the Bere Ferrers parish register he was baptised on 22 January 1777. Knighton confided to Letitia Treby that he was only twenty when Geach died, for reasons unknown stressing that the information was for her alone. However Geach died in February 1798 when, even allowing for a birth year of 1777, Knighton was at least twenty-one. Finally, in January 1832 Knighton observed that he had completed his fifty-fifth year on the fifth day of that month. If so, he was born in 1777. Dorothea was entirely mistaken about Knighton's volunteer service. First, she believed that he was a 'serjeant-major' which was a senior non-commissioned rank, beyond the competence of the nineteen-year-old Knighton and unlikely to have been given to the commanding officer's nephew-by-marriage. Secondly, she wrote that he resigned his commission because, when combined with his apprenticeship with Bredall, it encroached on his studies and overtaxed his strength. In reality Knighton retained his commission even when he was walking the wards in London. He did not resign until six months after his appointment to the Royal Naval Hospital.

As Knighton entered his twenties uncontroversial events were unaccountably misrepresented. The *Memoirs* implied that he was at the Royal Naval Hospital for only a few months, nine at most and certainly not the two-and-a-half years recorded in Creyke's journal. According to the obituary Knighton was never there at all, but on his return from London became a general practitioner in Tavistock. The confusion about Knighton's qualifications is so great that an unknown hand has attempted to amend Aberdeen University's copy of the *Memoirs*. Dorothea wrote that in 1797 Geach enabled Knighton to obtain a diploma from Aberdeen University for an essay on putrid fever, although *Munk's Roll*, a biographical dictionary of licentiates of the Royal College of Physicians, believed that the 1797 qualification was a Doctor of Medicine degree from St Andrews. However the resources of the Wellcome Library, with generous help from the archivists of St Andrews University, King's College Aberdeen, the Royal College of Physicians and Lambeth Palace, tell a slightly different story. St Andrews awarded Knighton an MD, or Doctor of Medicine degree, on 24 May 1800, the relevant minute noting that he had already received an AM. The latter was an honorary Master's degree, probably the diploma referred to in the *Memoirs*. On 21 April 1806 Knighton received a Doctor of Medicine degree from King's College, Aberdeen, and the Royal College of Physicians referred to the document that conferred his Aberdeen degree as a diploma. Knighton did not, as his obituary claimed, receive a degree from the Archbishop of Canterbury – an honorary 'Lambeth degree' – between leaving Edinburgh and becoming a Licentiate of the Royal College of Physicians.

Few aspects of Knighton's life are so conveniently documented. Dorothea wrote as though Knighton owned his Devonport home, but this is by no means certain. The address, 43 George Street, comes from his letter to Thomas Byam Martin of 1798. The George Street rate books do not survive. The rent books, which do, fail to mention him, so perhaps he occupied only part of the house. It is also possible that he did not live in Devonport for long. After George's death the provincial press reported that after practising in Devonport Knighton moved to Plymouth where he married Dorothea. There is similar uncertainty about his first attempt to establish himself in London. The *Memoirs* mentioned only his Argyll Street home, but in November 1803 Joseph Farington visited Dorothea at Princes Street, which is off the north-east corner of Hanover Square. *Boyle's Court Guide* for 1805, corrected up to 27 February of that year, listed a Dr Knighton at 10 Hanover Street; Hanover Street is off the south-east corner of Hanover Square, and No 10 was so close to the corner that it was almost in the square itself. Northcote's suspicion that the Knightons hoped to supplement their income with Dorothea's painting is strengthened by a modern suggestion that she was J Hawker, an honorary exhibitor at the Royal Academy between 1804 and 1809 whose paintings were engraved for topographical books. However it is compromised by Dorothea Lieven's allegation that Knighton poisoned his wife in 1802, and the fact that J Hawker the illustrator was styled 'Esq'. The obituary claimed that Knighton was later admonished by the Royal College of Physicians, not for uxoricide but for practising in London without a degree and that as a result he went to Edinburgh to study. Some accounts then omitted his purchase of 9 Hanover Square. According to Benjamin Brodie, when Knighton returned to London from Edinburgh he took a house in Maddox Street. Maddox Street was then south-east of Hanover Square – today's Maddox Street is longer – and its northern end still forms a near-apex with Hanover Street. A 1901 history of Hanover Square, which mistook the Reverend Sir Samuel Clarke Jervoise and his father for Admiral John Jervis, Earl St Vincent, who defeated the Spanish fleet in 1797, stated that Knighton practised as an accoucheur at 3 Tenterden Street, which lay near the north-west corner of Hanover Square within sight of No 9. According to this account Knighton was at first a tenant but later received No 3, fully furnished, in recognition of services rendered as an accoucheur in a 'delicate case'.

Knighton's connection with Sally Douglas made innuendo inevitable. One modern historian speculates whether Knighton came to Richard Wellesley's attention through Wellesley's connection with Bere Alston, but Wellesley had ceased to be a Member of Parliament for Bere Alston by 1790 when Knighton was at most fourteen. Hobhouse's version, written more than ten years after the Peninsula trip, was far more interesting. According to Hobhouse, Knighton 'contracted an intimacy' with Sally Douglas while in Plymouth. When Richard Wellesley wished to take Douglas to Spain she insisted on being accompanied by Knighton. At first Knighton did not want to go because he would lose fees, but eventually he agreed terms of £5,000 for two years, a suspiciously low figure. 'Mr. Perceval', however, prevented Douglas's trip, even though Spencer Perceval was at the time Chancellor of

Myth, Mistake and Discrepancy

the Exchequer and not yet Prime Minister. Hobhouse was perhaps misled by bad feeling between Richard Wellesley and Perceval over army funding for the Peninsula, but he was not wholly mistaken. Richard Wellesley wished to take a female companion to Spain but, as Iris Butler discovered from Hyacinthe's letters, she was a Miss Lesley or Leslie, not 'la Douglas'. Wellesley's plan was thwarted by Canning, then Foreign Secretary, after a plea from Hyacinthe. Nevertheless the poet Samuel Coleridge, writing to Robert Southey at some time between 26 October and 4 November 1809, was adamant that Sally Douglas was at that very moment with Richard Wellesley in Spain.

Hobhouse concluded his tale by saying that at the end of the mission Wellesley did not have enough money to pay Knighton, so by way of compensation introduced him to George and procured the promise of a baronetcy for him. The exact circumstances of the meeting are unclear. In later life Knighton wrote that he was asked to treat George's hand, but modern accounts diagnose George's ailment as a sprained ankle sustained while teaching his daughter the Highland fling. According to other rumours Knighton was not George's physician at all. A handwritten note at the top of the 1820 catalogue for Sherwood Lodge, presumably made at the time of sale, reads, 'Built by Mr Wolf a Dane or German in Wandsworth now the property of Sr Wm Knighton surgeon $^{?M.D.}$ to the late King' – that is, to George III who died on 29 January that year. The history of Hanover Square that placed Knighton at No 3 Tenterden Street claimed that George, when Prince Regent, appointed Knighton as physician to George III, for which services Knighton received £1,000 a year. People who by 1901 had lived in Hanover Square for more than fifty years – that is, they moved there about twenty years after Knighton sold No 9 – all told the same story – a doctor lived at 3 Tenterden Street and George III used to visit him there. There is no record of Knighton treating George III, but the rate books reveal that Robert Willis MD, who did, lived in Tenterden Street.

The history of Hanover Square implied that Knighton's baronetcy was granted because of his attendance on George III, while Raikes dated it from Knighton's role in retrieving McMahon's papers. Knighton's full title is also misrepresented. *Burke's Peerage* variously described him as Sir William Knighton of Carlston or Charlston, both in Dorset. As Timothy Duke of the College of Arms explains, this is almost certainly Charlestown, near Weymouth in Dorset. Its connection with Knighton has yet to be established. A year or so after receiving his baronetcy Knighton bought Sherwood Lodge, but both Knighton's contemporaries and modern historians have ignored his association with it. He undoubtedly lived there. *Underhill's Directory* recorded it as Knighton's address in 1817, albeit with the name misspelt. Gooch dreamed that he was there with Knighton and Dorothea, and both William and Mary Frances were baptised at St Mary's, Battersea.

The parish rates recorded Knighton as owner and occupier of Sherwood Lodge from 1814 to 1820, followed by Mrs Fitzherbert from 1821 to 1825. Fitzherbert's biographers however place her at Sherwood Lodge from the early 1810s following her final separation from George, and they have valid reasons for doing so. William Wilkins, who published in 1905, was lent a great many private papers, including those of the descendants of Fitzherbert's adopted daughter, and he was the first historian to study the Fitzherbert papers in the Royal Archives. His account included letters written to Fitzherbert at Sherwood Lodge in August 1812 and December 1816. The 1812 letter, from the Duke of York, was written when Sherwood Lodge was still owned by Wolff, and it is especially perplexing as it cannot be discounted as a letter to a visitor. York was glad that Fitzherbert was so pleased with Sherwood Lodge and felt so comfortable there. He was certain that it could be made 'very pretty', and he referred to having seen it with her on a previous occasion. Hindsight suggests that a home share between Knighton and Fitzherbert was unlikely. Greville claimed that Knighton, 'a stranger to Mrs. Fitzherbert', once called at her house – presumably on the pretext of enquiring after her health – and forced his way into her bedroom where she was ill in bed in an unsuccessful attempt to get hold of her private papers. Knighton for his part described Fitzherbert as 'an artful, cunning, designing woman, very selfish, with a temper of the worst description and a mind entirely under the influence of Popish superstition'. Hindsight however is not foolproof. Wilkins described Knighton's visit as occurring in Brighton in the 1820s, and Knighton wrote his opinion of Fitzherbert after George's death – it appears in Aspinall's *Letters*. A decade or so earlier relations may have been sufficiently cordial to allow short-term leases. There is a further twist, for the sales descriptions of 1820 and 1824 were very different. The 1820 advertisement – the Knighton sale – described Sherwood Lodge in detail. The 1824 advertisement – the Fitzherbert sale – claimed that words were inadequate to portray the 'distinguishing beauties' of Sherwood Lodge, and would reveal only that the interior decor reflected 'the excellent taste of the Proprietress' and that the grounds were a 'safe model whereon to guide others'. The 'dear cottage' has also been misrepresented. It became known as Blendworth Lodge – the first such reference is on a map of 1826 – and in a dictionary of architecture from 1848 Joseph Good's son wrote that Good 'designed and executed 1821-8 several works for the late Sir William Knighton, Bart., erecting a mansion for him at Horndean, Hampshire'. A modern architectural dictionary has interpreted this as meaning that Good built Blendworth Lodge. However Seymour's biography stated that Knighton bought a small house which he gradually enlarged. The mansion built for Knighton at Blendworth was Cadlington, a new build. Blendworth Lodge was an extension of an existing property.

Not all the discrepancies are inconsequential. Harriette Wilson wrote that when her sister Fanny was dying, the doctors in attendance were Sir William Knighton and a 'Sir John Millman' – to preserve the spontaneity of Harriette's writing her publisher prohibited her from revising her manuscripts, and she probably meant Sir Francis Milman, Knighton's 'particular friend' at the Royal College of Physicians. Harriette watched over Fanny at night, and a modern work states that while Knighton was attending Fanny he was guilty of sexual impropriety for which he subsequently paid blackmail money to Harriette. An alternative account, which holds that Fanny died not, as Harriette wrote, in an apartment in Brompton but in a nearby venereal diseases hospital, and that Harriette was not at Fanny's bedside but in Paris, might provide an alibi for Knighton, were not the author Harriette's former friend and later rival, the not wholly reliable Julia Johnstone. The accusation must remain yet another that is unlikely but which has yet to be disproved.

The most controversial event of Knighton's second career was his retrieval of McMahon's papers in August 1817. Richard Meade, third Earl of Clanwilliam, was a Foreign Office official and diplomat during the 1810s and 1820s. Meade believed that Knighton was recommended to McMahon by a Colonel Armstrong, whom Knighton had met in the Peninsula and who, incidentally, was one of Harriette Wilson's set. Meade's account corroborates both Knighton's statement that the McMahons cultivated his friendship while Richard Wellesley was Foreign Secretary – that is, between late 1809 and January 1812 – and Richard Wellesley's observation of 3 January 1812 that Knighton's qualities were already well known to McMahon. Meade wrote that Knighton treated McMahon for the two years in which McMahon was often deranged, and that when McMahon was ill he sent messages to George via Knighton, which would explain Knighton's contact with George in the mid-1810s when he was not active as physician-in-ordinary. According to Meade, on one occasion Knighton discovered McMahon strewing papers about his room, so he collected them, sealed them up and took them to George, who many years later told a guest at the Pavilion that Knighton's behaviour towards McMahon had always been 'most honourable'.

However Meade's opinion was not the consensus. McMahon died at Bath on 12 September 1817, and on 15 October *The Times* printed details of his will, naming one of his half-brothers, William, as his executor and describing Knighton's legacy as £500 'to another medical attendant'. However the later and universal assumption that McMahon's executor was Knighton, who came across or got hold of the papers after McMahon's death, was understandable. Knighton recorded in his journal entry of November

1830 that on learning of McMahon's death he went to Bath, got the will, and took it to George. The legend was born. Knighton's obituary, written nearly twenty years later, said that he was McMahon's executor, and that in the course of his executor's duties he found papers relating to George's private affairs. Opinion then differed as to whether, as the obituary stated, Knighton returned the papers 'without comment or condition' to George, who was impressed by his integrity, or whether he used them to blackmail George, who bought Knighton's silence with money and positions.

To protect George, Knighton let his contemporaries believe the worst, and perhaps even Dorothea did not know the truth. Knighton's letter to George of August 1817 makes it clear that Knighton retrieved papers from McMahon during McMahon's lifetime and with George's knowledge. However Knighton's account of November 1830, from the journal on which Dorothea based the *Memoirs*, omitted his visits to McMahon at Blackheath in August 1817. George was ambivalent about the episode. Harriett Arbuthnot's journal entry for 29 October 1823 recorded a recent conversation between George and her husband, Charles. George told Charles Arbuthnot that after McMahon's death Knighton sought an audience at which he announced that he knew all George's secret affairs. Taking the hint, George had given Knighton a draft for £25,000, only to be told that it was not enough. Knighton wanted a further £25,000 and Bloomfield's post at the Duchy of Cornwall, so George had to pay £12,000 for an annuity to compensate Bloomfield, making a total of £62,000. Hobhouse, writing in September 1821, recorded that Knighton had refused to hand over McMahon's papers without payment 'at an extravagant rate'. He wanted Bloomfield's post at the Duchy of Cornwall – Hobhouse wrongly believed that Bloomfield held the senior post of Receiver – and so an annuity was arranged for Bloomfield at a cost of £20,000 or £25,000 from the Privy Purse. Again, Hobhouse was not wholly mistaken. According to the figures in Knighton's letter to George of 16 December 1817, Bloomfield's annuity cost about £20,000.

Sir William Knighton

Dorothea Lieven believed that Knighton's knowledge caused George to fear him and that the fear bred a strange dependency. Harriett Arbuthnot, who not infrequently described Knighton as a rogue and blackguard, wrote that he told George 'every gossiping story of every house in London'. Arthur Wellesley had begged her not to seek medical advice from Knighton who, he claimed, regaled George with the complaints of his women patients. According to Francis Conyngham, Elizabeth Conyngham's middle son, by the late 1820s George was expressing loudly and within earshot of his pages a heartfelt wish that someone would assassinate Knighton. Nevertheless it seemed to Greville, to whom Francis Conyngham told the story, that there was 'some secret chain' that bound George and Knighton together, although Greville also believed that George was a slave to habit and would retain people he disliked rather than adapt to change. Knighton's influence over George was perceived by some as inappropriate and by others as a blessing. As early as Christmas 1822 Arthur Wellesley was resigned to the fact that nothing could be decided until Knighton's return, and by 1823 Hobhouse believed that Elizabeth Conyngham and Knighton had 'an almost entire control' over George. However in 1829 Greville observed that Knighton was still the only man who could prevail on George to sign papers and attend to business, while Andrew Dickie of Coutts recalled that when large bills for unbudgeted expenditure arrived 'like thunder-claps ... Sir William's words, tone, and manner acted like magic upon the King'.

Although Knighton was renowned for his tact and impeccable courtesy Dorothea Lieven described him as having 'sharp eyes'. On one occasion Knighton smiled at her when she flattered George and she did not know whether he was laughing with her or at her. As Hobhouse noted, Knighton was considered a 'damned clever fellow'. Greville wrote that Knighton managed George's affairs well and got him out of debt. Hobhouse observed that Knighton was more assiduous than his predecessors in collecting the Duchies' revenues but believed that this was because Knighton had a scheme to make George financially independent of the Government. Knighton's own wealth was said by Raikes to be prodigious, and Hobhouse was told that Knighton was obsessed with the price of stocks. Creevey was certain that a hefty bill for erecting tents at Virginia Water included a percentage for Knighton's work, while Raikes believed that both McMahon and Knighton profited from inside information. Harriett Arbuthnot was certain that Knighton abused privileged information to engage in illicit speculation. She blamed a fall in the value of Government securities in July 1824 on Knighton's gambling 'in the funds' – funds were Government bonds that raised finance to run the country and whose interest was paid by taxation – and both she and her husband believed that Knighton would use a forthcoming trip to Barèges as an excuse to visit Paris and gamble in the French funds.

Knighton was frequently said to be George's private secretary, even though the post was officially abolished in 1822. The obituary and *Munk's Roll* perpetuated the error and even Knighton's contemporaries believed it. Recalling Bloomfield's activities, Harriett Arbuthnot wondered how George would explain to Knighton that his duties included buying up incriminating caricatures and newspaper reports about Elizabeth Conyngham and George. Eight months before the Milan Commission was appointed Knighton was monitoring provincial newspapers, and he perhaps progressed to intervention. In January 1822 Hobhouse suspected that Knighton had instigated flattering reports about Richard Wellesley and disparaging ones about Bloomfield, while in early 1824 Elizabeth Fox, the hostess of Holland House, attributed unflattering articles about Elizabeth Conyngham to Knighton's withdrawal of the customary hush money to editors. Aspinall believed that Knighton manipulated the press on George's behalf, while Walter Scott advised his son-in-law, the new editor of the *Quarterly Review*, that the 'gallipot' – an old-fashioned glazed medicine bottle – was 'accessible'. A likely example of Knighton's intervention occurred during the Harriette Wilson crisis of 1827, when a report that Knighton was on his way to Paris on a secret mission, and that such journeys were not infrequent, was followed by another explaining that Knighton's journeys were 'to purchase ornamental furniture for his Majesty, which could not be obtained in England'. For good measure it added that all other items had been made by British craftsmen. The press however was not easily duped. A report of March 1828 at the time of the de Beaune affair, stating that Knighton was on his way to Hanover because of the continued and serious indisposition of the Duke of Cambridge, was contradicted by another declaring that Cambridge was in perfect health and had been so for a considerable time. A popular theory held that Knighton had left the country because he had been denounced by Thomas Duncombe but, as Croker noted, Knighton frequently went abroad.

Attempts to manipulate human behaviour can yield unintended consequences. Thomas Duncombe's speech of February 1828 upset Knighton more than any other attack. However a week later Greville recorded in his journal that the whole speech was an obscure joke written for Duncombe by an aristocratic society wit who considered the young Member of Parliament a fool. If so, only the author was amused. The speech was taken seriously and earned for Knighton the sinister epithet of 'the invisible' which he never shed. However after George's death politically motivated criticism worried him less. His life now centred on the country cottage retirement that he had deferred for more than twenty years.

Chapter 11
1830–1836: Retirement

The Blendworth of 'home and sincerity and affection' to which Knighton flew in the summer of 1830 had changed as the younger generation reached adulthood and the older sought promotion. Reverend Charles Boyles was no longer the Reverend Sir Samuel's curate, for he had recently secured a comfortable living in a nearby parish where he was now living with his mother. His aunt Elizabeth, whose husband had died at Blendworth in 1820, rented Boyles' property, Green Hook. Elizabeth's son, Edward Osborn, ordained the previous year and newly married, was living locally, probably at Hook Cottage, and from March 1831 he signed the Blendworth vestry minutes as minister or curate. Seymour, Commissioner for Portsmouth Dockyard since 1829, had moved with 'her dearest Ladyship' to an opulent official residence in the Dockyard from where he was soon able to marry off one of his seven daughters. Meanwhile he let Blendworth House to one Edmond Waller Rundell, whose distinctive but frequently misspelt name identifies him as the second and recently-retired Rundell in Rundell, Bridge & Rundell, George's jewellers. Cadlington House was complete, and in 1832 Dora and Michael baptised their second child, Georgina. Blendworth Cottage was being enlarged piecemeal, probably to accommodate Knighton's art collection.

The next two years were mostly happy and healthy for Knighton. Loath to make a complete break with his second career, he retained his posts for life at the Duchies of Cornwall and Lancaster. Their combined income of around £2,000 was useful but not essential, and he was perhaps more concerned to protect John Tolle's deputy-receiverships. Knighton's responsibilities as George's executor also required his presence in London, but trips to town were now a pleasant complement to domesticity. In London in October 1830 to call on his fellow executor, Arthur Wellesley, and meet Dickie on Duchy business, Knighton became the archetypal country squire in a trip to town. He called on David Wilkie at Kensington, viewed his current work and discussed William Wellesley's painting and artistic talent in general, privately disagreeing with Wilkie's assertion that the latter was mostly a matter of application to drudgery. In the evening he went with an unnamed companion to a bookseller in Pall Mall to order 'several instructive books of art' – Knighton would never regard painting as a leisure activity – and on the spur of the moment joined a stream of people filling the church of St Mary le Strand opposite Somerset House. In what would become a preoccupation, Knighton noted the preacher's reminder that even the greatest saints were liable to occasional sin, but the newly-freed Knighton, healthy enough to make most of these journeys on foot, had yet to be tormented by contemplation of his past actions. The following morning he walked to the studio of painter John Linnell at Bayswater. Twenty years earlier Knighton had recorded his delight at being included in the witty conversations of Richard Wellesley. Now he relished the company of Linnell who allowed him a privileged sight of images by Holbein and Raphael. It was the stuff of these works, said Linnell, that kept the mind on fire.

In late afternoon Knighton treated himself to a meal at Dolly's Chophouse, an ancient and out-of-the-way, no-nonsense purveyor of beefsteak and ale near St Paul's. By the time he finished his meal it was dusk, and he crossed the graveyard to the cathedral, paid his two pence and went in, only to be disappointed. Earlier that year Knighton had recorded in his diary his disgust that Arthur Wellesley saw no merit in civilian service. He now surveyed St Paul's memorials in the fading light and concluded that by and large they commemorated the 'accidental circumstance' of being in the wrong place at the wrong time in a battle. With some difficulty he found three exceptions – Samuel Johnson, writer and man of words; Joshua Reynolds, the portrait painter under whom Northcote studied and first president of the Royal Academy; and John Howard, prison reformer. Knighton's admiration for Howard was unreserved.

1830–1836: Retirement

To engage in pleasantries with the hero of Waterloo and sometime Prime Minister was none the less gratifying, and Knighton recorded verbatim some small-talk from a meeting with Arthur Wellesley of November 1830. Although Knighton became increasingly didactic he remained a sociable man. He enjoyed the company of young people, and on a visit to town in May 1832 he spent time with William and 'John'. With no London house Knighton at first stayed at Limmer's, which must have improved since Captain Gronow described it as the dirtiest hotel in London. However the 'repetition of fame' to which Knighton once attributed his success was not, as he once believed, perpetual. The May visit included the Christie's sale of pictures belonging to the late Henry Phipps, Lord Mulgrave, who as First Lord of the Admiralty had in 1808 presented Seymour with the King's medal for capturing *La Thetis*, and whose private patronage had encouraged Wilkie. By 1834 Knighton's health was too uncertain for hotel life and in July that year he took a lease on 14 Stratford Place, off Oxford Street, as a London base for the rest of the family.

One of the early nineteenth century's more pleasant forms of medical treatment was 'carriage exercise', and in his first years of retirement Knighton travelled in Europe for pleasure and health with companions of his choice. His trip to Paris in early spring 1831, though involving delivery of a letter to an elderly Frenchman from an English aristocrat, both unnamed, was to see the sights, look at pictures and perhaps come home with a bargain or two. He complained of deteriorating eyesight but, healthier than he had been for years, casually mentioned walking to the lens maker to have his spectacles changed. In London Knighton had considered it prudent to decline invitations to dine, but in Paris he and his companion ate at a restaurant every day. Trained by Geach to observe, Knighton compulsively recorded the foibles of his fellow man, noting how the coxcomb twirled his mustachio to signify self-satisfaction. Still a romantic, Knighton saw in two young lovers at dinner, indifferent to the food before them, 'the sensibilities of the best part of our nature'.

In observing others Knighton revealed the values that he held in late middle age. They were moderation, social order, paternalism and the

Protestant religion. He relished being mystified as to why it took four French officials to examine his passport. More seriously, he believed that the mass of French people craved an annual dose of excitement which they sought under the pretext of liberty, and that only military power could govern them. They were intelligent and resourceful and in some respects more honest than the English but, he reasoned, these qualities were countermanded by vanity, which rendered the French lacking in judgment; his observation that French soldiers were regardless of danger and unquestioningly loyal to a trusted leader was therefore less than complimentary. He regarded the French as irreligious, with no core of ideals to restrain their conduct. They had rejected what he called the 'superficial worship' of Roman Catholicism and were ready to adopt Protestantism but, Knighton was informed, the Jesuits used female servants to infiltrate family households in an attempt to regain political power. In September 1831 Knighton, again accompanied by an unnamed companion, arrived in Paris during a mob protest. The previous year the French had deposed the direct descendant of their twice-restored Bourbon dynasty in favour of a more distant relation. This year the protest was against the failure of the French government to support the Poles against their czarist rulers. Despite his own brush with the Holy Alliance Knighton dismissed the protest as a 'Jacobinical brawl'. Parisians, he noted, were easily subdued by the presence of troops and welcomed any opportunity for idleness – he had already noted the closed shops.

As Knighton was uncomfortably aware, protest was not an exclusively French pastime. The predilection for disorder that he condemned in France came to London in the form of agitation for reform of Parliament and public life. The movement had started in the late eighteenth century, and Knighton's dispute with the Royal College of Physicians had been a symptom. In November 1830 Arthur Wellesley caused a fall in the funds, created fear of riots and was forced to resign as Prime Minister after expressing perfect satisfaction with the existing system of Parliamentary representation and announcing his intention to oppose its reform. During the severe winter of 1830 to 1831 Hampshire landowners reduced their rents and clergymen their tithes to alleviate hardship, but resentment against the established order continued. In June 1831 the *Hampshire Telegraph* reported that Michael, Reverend Sir Samuel's eldest son, Jervoise, and another local gentleman were to raise a local yeomanry corps, a cavalry equivalent of the volunteer infantry corps in which Knighton had served at Tavistock. The former was currently without a ship and the latter was without an occupation, and the *Telegraph*, published in reformist Portsmouth, stated that as the object of the corps was mutual protection, its expenses should be met by the individuals involved. Government help should be limited to the supply of arms.

Finding himself alone in London in October 1831 after the second of three reform Bills introduced that year had been rejected by a large majority in the Lords, Knighton recorded with disgust that shops were shut as though it were a Sunday, and that tradesmen, journeymen and labourers were on the streets and refusing to work. Hindsight makes Knighton's opposition to reform seem illogical. Public criticism of him had been caused by the ambivalence of his work for George – he had acted without pay as George's private secretary, a post that was supposed to have been abolished, and received public money for his Duchy posts, which many regarded as near sinecures. Reform of public life would root out anomalies, establishing clear pay and responsibilities. However, isolated in a London that seemed to be populated by Parisians, Knighton equated reform with revolution and opposed it. The farmer's son who as a teenager had read a borrowed copy of Pope from cover to cover and chosen a travel book instead of a new suit of clothes now blamed 'the blessings of too much education' for placing workers 'quite beyond their once happy sphere of life'. The four-year-old who was said to have narrowly escaped the parish charity was now a middle-aged landowner, angered and frightened by press reports of riots, deaths and arson, who bemoaned the state of his 'once happy country'.

A few years ago any one of these events would have brought a royal messenger to Blendworth or a carriage to the door of 9 Hanover Square. Now they were other people's concerns. Knighton was more interested in his ambitions for William who graduated from Oxford in May 1831.

According to James Dafforne, a nineteenth-century writer on art, William first studied under Thomas Lawrence. Knighton believed that William had inherited his, Knighton's, artistic sensibilities and Dorothea's practical skill, and he approved his son's choice as 'an occupation at once innocent and intellectual'. Financially independent, William would be spared the vagaries of public life yet would know the discipline of study and application. In January 1832 William travelled to Paris to attend a studio, accompanied by Knighton who was to stay while his son settled in. Within a fortnight Knighton had left his hotel suite for William's 'little lodging', run by a kind and helpful widow, clean and, despite its perilously well-waxed red tiles, comfortable. What more, observed Knighton, could one desire? Having been unwell in Paris, he even managed to praise the tiles as a reminder of life's ups and downs. At the end of March 'dear John' brought William's portfolio to Blendworth, from where Knighton had been issuing fatherly advice and homilies of the nose-to-the-grindstone variety. When William returned to England he studied with David Wilkie, who had long taken an interest in his progress, and attended a Bloomsbury drawing academy highly regarded by Wilkie and described by its proprietor as a probationary school for the Royal Academy. In March 1834 Wilkie reported to Knighton that William was getting closer to realising on paper and canvas what he imagined in his head, and the following month William was accepted as a student of the Royal Academy.

Despite Knighton's illness of January 1832 he undertook two long trips in England that year. One was to Devon and old haunts. At Devonport he went out at dusk to see his old house – his journal failed to mention that No 43 George Street was demolished in 1811 to enlarge the Port Admiral's garden. Once there Knighton recalled his former self with an inexplicable horror yet found no satisfaction in his subsequent achievements. Earlier memories, however, were happy. He enjoyed walking the familiar lanes and hedgerows around Newton Bushell, the location of his much-despised school. Travelling up the Tamar from Devonport to Hole's Hole on the west shore of Bere Ferrers, from where Lockeridge produce was sent to

Plymouth, he recognised spots he had known as a boy, a rare admission that he was ever a child. Betraying his local origins, he recorded not just that he saw fishermen but that they were trying for salmon. He stayed at the home of Thamzin, his sister, but was ill at ease. The next day he visited Dorothy's grave. Unsurprisingly he was comforted there. Surprisingly, given Bere Ferrers' steep hills, he walked the three miles plus to the church. In the autumn of 1832 he was fit and active.

The year of 1832 was not however without anxiety. Parliamentary representation was only one aspect of British life subject to reform, and Knighton's family were directly affected by changes in naval administration. Rumours appeared in the Portsmouth press in December 1831, and in 1832 Dockyard Commissioners' jobs for life were abolished, renamed and given to serving officers. According to his biography, in early June Seymour was summoned to the Admiralty and offered two options. Under the first he could continue as Commissioner for another three years and retire with a civil pension. Alternatively he could be reinstated as a naval officer with the rank he would have had had he not resigned, and become head of the South America station at Rio. Given the choice of remaining at Portsmouth with a guaranteed pension in three years' time, or sailing to the other side of the world to a climate that had nearly killed him as a young man but where he could help his sons' careers, the sixty-four-year-old Seymour chose Rio. He tried unsuccessfully to have Michael appointed captain of his flagship, the *Spartiate*, but he was able to take his fourth son, Edward, as lieutenant. At Knighton's request Brougham, now Lord Chancellor, approached the First Lord of the Admiralty, and Michael went to Rio as captain of his own ship, the *Challenger*, with a cousin, James Luscombe, as a midshipman. Seymour arrived in Rio in April 1833 and almost immediately became ill, but in January 1834 he claimed to feel better and wrote that he hoped 'to settle down into a quiet old country gentleman by the year 1837'. The *Memoirs* said nothing of Knighton's emotions on parting from the man who had been his friend for more than thirty years or of the conversations between them. Knighton's writings, however, became increasingly sombre. His journal for a trip to Wales with Dickie in June 1833 recorded a sermon at a Nonconformist chapel in Bath. The preacher described with heartbreaking realism the miseries that Christians must endure during their sorrowful probationary lives on earth before attaining the peace of heaven. As he spoke of the loss of a child – 'perhaps an only child' – he appeared to Knighton to be close to tears, but he assured his congregation that saints and Christians would know each other in heaven, and that all the children who had died before their time were waiting in heaven to welcome their Christian parents. Knighton was deeply moved but remained easily dispirited. He was at first charmed by a country churchyard whose graves were planted with box, rosemary and wild flowers. All was well until Knighton read the tombstone of a young man who had died two years ago leaving a widow and child. The grave was freshly tended and covered with blooms, and Knighton began to think that he too would like to be buried in this churchyard, with his beloved children showing their love by planting flowers on his grave and tending it thereafter, perhaps helped by his infant granddaughters. His thoughts then moved swiftly from graves to death and to perpetual separation from his children and grandchildren, and he ended with a prayer that God would preserve them all.

The *Memoirs* failed to record that during the first years of Knighton's retirement he was periodically attacked in the press as a symbol of the bad old days. In April 1831 a letter to *The Times* included Knighton in an exposé of sinecures and called the Duchy of Lancaster 'a nest of jobbing'. *The Extraordinary Black Book* for 1832 suggested that Knighton might usefully employ his leisure explaining to 'the burthened community' the exact nature of services to the Crown provided by numerous females in receipt of Court pensions. In February 1833 *The Times* criticised the Duchy of Cornwall, identifying its Deputy-Receiver as 'John Toll' and describing him as 'Sir William Knighton's near relative'. However Knighton was no longer involved in matters of state. When the Prime Minister resigned in July 1834 the only consequence for Knighton was a stay in London in case a new Chancellor of the Duchy of Lancaster was appointed. After a routine

1830–1836: Retirement

signing of Duchy accounts in June 1835, the former Duke of Clarence, now William IV and no longer dependent on Knighton's powers of intercession, invited Knighton to stay at Windsor. Writing to Mary Frances from the castle, Knighton reported that although the King and Queen had been gracious and attentive and treated him with kindness and distinction, he felt as though the late King was still lying dead in his chamber.

The difficulties that beset Knighton were no longer those of a bright boy with a poor education, or of a young doctor dogged by family mysteries, or of a loyal servant to a charming but idle and capricious royal master. They were those of middle-aged Everyman. His old friends began to fall ill and die. In April 1831 Walter Scott, prone to strokes, suffered a seizure from which he never fully recovered. Northcote died in July 1831 aged eighty-five. Despite the *Memoirs*' assurance that Northcote's autobiography was in the press, Knighton never got round to editing the manuscript, and it remained in the family until William's death. In November 1831 Knighton attended his old friend, Charles Sumner, who was dangerously ill with fever but who recovered to outlive Knighton by many years. In March 1834 Knighton paid a last visit to Dickie. George Harrison came with him but was unable to get out of the carriage.

While Knighton was spending more and more time at Blendworth, an old acquaintance was, as Richard Culpin explains, preparing to leave. Around 1832 Reverend Sir Samuel Clarke Jervoise and his wife decided to live permanently in London, and in February 1835 Reverend Sir Samuel formally settled Idsworth on their eldest son, Jervoise, who was by then married with a family. On 5 November 1834, Samuel's last day as master of Idsworth, Jervoise wrote in his diary, 'Sir W. Knighton called to take leave, friendly as usual to one & all yesterday.' However Samuel's departure had unintended consequences for Knighton's family. Because Samuel was leaving the area he gave up his local livings, including the living at Blendworth. Patronage of the livings – the right to appoint their rectors – had been sold in the executors' sale of Thomas Clarke Jervoise. Reverend Sir Samuel nevertheless retained the right to remain rector, and while he did so Edward Osborn was minister in all but name. By 1830 the patron of the Blendworth living was the Reverend Edward Ward. A former naval chaplain who had seen the slave trade at first hand in the West Indies and was a committed abolitionist, Ward had much in common with the Knightons and Seymours. However he had had his own reasons for buying a living with a sixty-year-old incumbent. In October 1834 Ward appointed one of his sons, Reverend Edward Langton Ward, as Blendworth's Rector. Unfortunately Reverend Edward Langton Ward intended to administer his parish in person. Awaiting the new Rector, Osborn, who had formerly signed the Vestry Minutes as curate, pointedly wrote 'inhabitant'.

In retrospect Ward's arrival would prove the least of Knighton's worries. In May 1834 Seymour wrote home to say that he had been seriously ill but that he was now recovering. Nevertheless, explaining that as 'people do not die one minute sooner for making a Will', he had made one. There was no further news until early September, when Knighton was called from dinner at Blendworth. When he returned he was, in Dorothea's words, 'pale, and dreadfully agitated'. Seymour had died in July. Knighton never fully recovered from the news. In January 1835 he wrote that his pulse was erratic, and he attributed the change to the shock of Seymour's death combined with a severe cold and asthmatic attack that lasted several weeks. Believing that the change was 'the forerunner of sudden death', he decided to live from month to month and avoid 'the excitements of emotion'.

While Knighton endeavoured to preserve his life, he prepared his soul for death. For a conservative man his choice of religious instruction was unusual. He read the journal of George Whitefield, an eighteenth-century Anglican clergyman turned Evangelical, and concurred with Whitefield's belief in Providence – that is, in God's intervention in human life for specific reasons. He also read Caroline Fry, an educated, middle-class convert to Evangelism, and the Knightons' contemporary in London, where she was part of society. Trips to London on business became opportunities to hear sermons which he discussed in his journal. He was drawn to Evangelicals and clergymen who were active in their congregations. Rowland Hill was

1830–1836: Retirement

denied preferment in the Church of England for refusing to give up itinerant preaching but used an inheritance to build a chapel in south London where he established Sunday schools. Henry Blunt of Chelsea influenced the rich while making religious study available to the poor. Reverend Sanderson Robins of Maida Vale, a tolerant Anglican dedicated to the education and care of poor children, became a close friend. Despite his preoccupation with religion, Knighton lost none of his shrewdness, and when a number of small fields, shops and cottages in Blendworth were offered for sale in 1835, Knighton bought his pick of them. However by now his health was so precarious that any shock, even that of tragedy averted, made him ill. In October 1835 Knighton received a letter from Michael and learned that his beloved son-in-law had been shipwrecked, menaced by natives, endangered by earthquakes and was now at sea on his way to Portsmouth to face a court martial for losing the *Challenger*. James Luscombe, who was aboard as a midshipman, was not among the dead, but the *Hampshire Telegraph* reported that the crew's 'young gentlemen' formed a large proportion of the sick. In the event the *Challenger*'s crew were treated as heroes for surviving their ordeal and Michael was exonerated. The *Telegraph* reported that never before had 'so large an assemblage of ladies' attended a naval court martial, adding that they belonged to 'the most fashionable families in the neighbourhood'. Knighton's spirits lifted for a while as he awaited the providential blessing that he was sure Michael's ordeal would prove to be.

On 5 January 1836, his birthday, Knighton doubted whether he would have another but felt ill-prepared for death. He rallied, however, when planning William's career as an artist, and as late as July 1836 had not entirely given up hopes of travelling abroad with him. A loving, gossipy letter of 17 July 1836 to William was Knighton's last contribution to the *Memoirs*. William was about to arrive for an extended stay at Blendworth, and Knighton was making plans. Oblivious or indifferent to her family's local notoriety, he had arranged for a gipsy, Mary Stanley, to visit Blendworth to sit for William. He would go to the nearby beach at Hayling Island three times a week to get the sea air, and William could go swimming. In the last paragraph Knighton reported that Dora and her new baby, a third daughter, were doing well. He ended with a blessing for William and signed himself 'ever, Your most affectionate and attached parent'.

Thereafter the narrative passed to Dorothea. Knighton spent a final summer at Blendworth, far from well but surrounded by his family, happy to sit in William's studio, enjoying his son's company and watching the progress of *The Gipsy Girl*. However his signature on a lease in August appears to have been made with difficulty, and that month his breathing became so laboured that he went to London for medical advice, only to deteriorate on his return. After a particularly harrowing night Dorothea and William persuaded him to risk going back to London to be near Tupper and Chambers. In London he put his affairs in order, and people for whom he felt affection were gathered round him. His will of 1 September was witnessed by three servants whose surnames had Blendworth connections. A codicil of 6 September was witnessed by Thamzin and one, possibly two, of her daughters. The will's only surprise was a bequest to Michael of the Blendworth properties that Knighton had bought the previous summer. On 12 September he assigned the lease of No 14 to William. His family provided for, Knighton's depression seemed to Dorothea to lift.

In the closing pages of the *Memoirs*' penultimate chapter, Dorothea recorded what she believed were Knighton's emotions during the last weeks of his life, and she reconciled the conflicting demands of duty to one's King and to an all-powerful, infinitely good and loving God, who arranged every incident of life for good reason. She forestalled criticism of Knighton by revealing that he believed himself to be a sinner, and one statement which she attributed to him was especially startling. According to Dorothea, shortly before Knighton died he told a 'kind relative', 'When I was a young man, I knew God; but I departed from Him, and he [sic] has brought me back to Himself again.' Dorothea reminded her readers that Knighton had had to perform 'many an unsatisfactory service' – in other words, by serving his King, Knighton had imperilled his soul. The 'undeserved censure and enmity' that he had suffered may have shortened his life but his attackers were, she reasoned, 'the instruments of his [God's] controlling power' and part of God's plan.

Knighton spent his last days surrounded by his children and by people whom Dorothea did not name but whom she described as 'many near relatives who were sincerely attached to him'. She described a prayer that he said with a friend in which he asked that, if he were not to be made well, he might be given 'a sense of sin, and of peace in joy of his Saviour'. He had at last realised the futility of judging himself and found the Christian resignation that he believed had eluded Gooch. On Saturday, 8 October Knighton received Holy Communion from Edward Osborn, and he died three days later. Dorothea's description of his death is that of a man at peace. As Knighton had explained to Anne Grey many years earlier, he believed that after death the human soul took bodily form but, because it no longer had to sustain bodily needs, the only emotion it needed was love. It was no longer obliged to think.

Illustrations

(above) Feather by Mrs Dorothea Knighton, c1801
Copyright Plymouth and West Devon Record Office, 864/7

(above) Sherwood Lodge, anon, 1810
Copyright The Georgian Group Pardoe Collection, LON008

Sir William Knighton

Blendworth House by Lady Knighton, 1820s
Copyright The Georgian Group Pardoe Collection, HANTS004

Illustrations

'The Jew and the doctor; or, secret Influence behind the Curtain!! Vide Times Feby. 19th. 1828', 1828
Copyright British Museum, AN178784001, BM satires 15522

153

Sir William Knighton

View of Hole's Hole Quay on the Tamar by the Reverend John Swete, 1793
Copyright Devon Record Office 564M/F3/124

SELECT BIBLIOGRAPHY

Letters and diaries

Aspinall, A. (editor), *Letters of King George IV, 1812–1830*, 3 volumes (Cambridge: Cambridge University Press, 1938)

Aspinall, A. (editor), *The Correspondence of Charles Arbuthnot*, Camden Society Publications, 3rd series, No 65 (London: The Royal Historical Society, 1941)

Aspinall, A. (editor), *The Diary of Henry Hobhouse, 1820–1827* (London: Home and Van Thal, 1947)

Aspinall, A., *The Correspondence of George, Prince of Wales, 1770–1810*, 8 volumes (London: Cassell, 1963–1971)

Bamford, Francis, and the Duke of Wellington (editors), *The Journal of Mrs. Arbuthnot, 1820–1832*, 2 volumes (London: Macmillan, 1950)

Fletcher, Ernest, *Conversations of James Northcote R.A. with James Ward, on Art and Artists. Edited and arranged from the manuscripts and notebooks of James Ward* (London: Methuen and Co., 1901)

Ford, John M. T. (editor), *Medical History,* Supplement No 7, *A Medical Student at St Thomas's Hospital, 1801–1802. The Weekes Family Letters* (London: Wellcome Institute for the History of Medicine, 1987)

Garlick, Kenneth, Angus Macintyre and others (editors), *The Diary of Joseph Farington,* 17 volumes (New Haven and London: Yale University Press, 1978–1998)

Gates, Eleanor M., *Leigh Hunt: A Life in Letters, Together With Some Correspondence of William Hazlitt* (Essex, Connecticut: Falls River Publications, c1998)

Gore, John (editor), *Creevey* (London: John Murray, revised edition 1948)

Grieg, James (editor), *The Farington Diary*, 8 volumes (London: Hutchinson and Co., 1922–1928)

Grierson, H. J. C., Davidson Cook, W. M. Parker and others, *The Letters of Sir Walter Scott*, volumes 7–11 of 12 (London: Constable, 1934–1937)

Griggs, E. L. (editor), *Collected Letters of Samuel Taylor Coleridge,* volume

3 of 4 (Oxford: Clarendon Press, 1959)

Ilchester, the Earl of (editor), *Elizabeth, Lady Holland, to her Son, 1821–1845* (London: John Murray, 1946)

Jennings, Louis J. (editor), *The Croker Papers. The Correspondence and Diaries of the late Right Honourable John Wilson Croker*, 2nd edition, volume 1 of 3 (London: John Murray, 1885)

Kriegel, Abraham D. (editor), *The Holland House Diaries, 1831–1840. The Diary of Henry Holland Vassall Fox, third Lord Holland, with extract from the diary of Dr. John Allen* (London, Henley and Boston: Routledge and Kegan Paul, 1977)

Marchand, Leslie A. (editor), *Byron's Letters and Journals*, volume 4 of 13 (London: John Murray, 1975)

Meade, Richard: see electronic sources

Morrison, Alfred, *The Collection of Autograph Letters and Historical Documents formed by Alfred Morrison*, 2nd series 1882–1893, 3 volumes A–D (Printed for private circulation 1893–1896)

Raikes, Thomas, *A Portion of the Journal kept by Thomas Raikes, Esq., from 1831 to 1847*, volume 3 of 4 (London: Longman, Brown, Green and Longmans, 1856)

Quennell, Peter (editor) and Dilys Powell (translator), *The Private Letters of Princess Lieven to Prince Metternich, 1820–1826*, (London: John Murray, Albermarle Library, 1948)

Thursfield, H. G. (editor), 'Peter Cullen Esq., 1789–1802', in *Five Naval Journals, 1789–1817* (London: Navy Records Society, 1951), pages 41–119

Wellington, the Seventh Duke of (editor), *Wellington and his Friends* (London: Macmillan, 1965)

Wellesley, F. A. (editor), *The Diary and Correspondence of Henry Wellesley, First Lord Cowley, 1790–1846* (London: Hutchinson & Co. Ltd, 1930)

Wilson, Philip Whitwell (editor), *The Greville Diary*, 2 volumes (London: William Heinemann, 1927)

Select bibliography

Biographical

Blainey, Ann, *Immortal Boy. A Portrait of Leigh Hunt* (London and Sydney: Croom Helm, 1985)

Blanche, Lesley (editor), *Harriette Wilson's Memoirs* (London: Phoenix Press, 2003)

Bloomfield, Lady Georgiana (editor), *Memoir of Benjamin Lord Bloomfield*, 2 volumes (London: Chapman and Hall, 1884)

Brodie, Sir Benjamin C., *Autobiography of the late Sir Benjamin C. Brodie, Bart.*, 2nd edition (London: Longmans, Green, and Co., 1865)

Butler, Iris, *The Eldest Brother. The Marquess Wellesley, the Duke of Wellington's Eldest Brother* (London: Hodder and Stoughton, 1973)

Cunningham, Allan, *The Life of Sir David Wilkie; with his Journals, Tours and Critical Remarks on Works of Art; and a Selection from his Correspondence,* 3 volumes (London: John Murray, 1843)

Dafforne, James, *Life and Works of Edward Matthew Ward, R.A.* (London: Virtue and Co. Ltd, 1879)

Fraser, Flora, *The Unruly Queen. The Life of Queen Caroline* (London and Basingstoke: Papermac, 1997)

Gronow, Rees Howell, *The Reminiscences and Recollections of Captain Gronow*, volume 1 of 2 (Nunney: The R. S. Surtees Society, 1984)

Gwynn, Stephen, *Memorials of an Eighteenth-Century Painter (James Northcote)* (London: T. Fisher Unwin, 1898)

Hibbert, Christopher, *George IV. Prince of Wales, 1762–1811* (Newton Abbot: Readers Union, 1973)

Hibbert, Christopher, *George IV. Regent and King, 1811–1830* (Newton Abbot: Readers Union, 1975)

Hinde, Wendy, *George Canning* (London: Collins, 1973)

Holmes, Timothy, *Sir Benjamin Collins Brodie* (London: T. Fisher Unwin, 1898)

Johnstone, Julia, *Confessions of Julia Johnstone. Written by Herself. In contradiction to the fables of Harriette Wilson* (London: Benbow, 1825)

Knighton, Lady [Dorothea], *Memoirs of Sir William Knighton, Bart.,*

G.C.H., *Keeper of the Privy Purse during the Reign of His Majesty King George the Fourth. Including his correspondence with many distinguished persons,* 2 volumes (London: Richard Bentley, 1838)

Le Marchant, Sir Denis, *Memoir of John Charles, Viscount Althorp, Third Earl Spencer* (London: Richard Bentley, 1876)

Leslie, C. R., and Tom Taylor, *Life and Times of Sir Joshua Reynolds,* 2 volumes (London: John Murray, 1865)

Macmichael, William, *Lives of British Physicians* (London: John Murray, 1830)

Morpurgo, J. E., *The Autobiography of Leigh Hunt* (London: The Cresset Press, 1949)

Pettigrew, Thomas Joseph, *Medical Portrait Gallery*, 4 volumes (London: Fisher, Son and Co., 1838–1840)

Pycroft, George, *Art in Devonshire: with the Biographies of Artists Born in that County* (Exeter: Henry S. Eland; London: Hamilton, Adams and Co., 1883)

Redford, George and John Angell James (editors), *The Autobiography of William Jay: with reminiscences of some distinguished contemporaries, selections from his correspondence, etc.* (London: Hamilton, Adams and Co., 1854)

Cameron, Kenneth Neill, and Donald H. Reiman, *Shelley and his Circle, 1773–1822,* 8 volumes (Cambridge, Massachusetts: Harvard University Press, 1973)

Seymour, Richard, *Memoir of Rear-Admiral Sir Michael Seymour, Bart., K.C.B.* (Printed by Spottiswoode and Co., London, 1878. Not published.)

Stapleton, Augustus Granville, *George Canning and his Times* (London: John W. Parker and Son, 1859)

Stapleton, Augustus Granville, *The Political Life of Mr. Canning*, 2 volumes (London: Longman, Fees, Orme, Brown, and Green: 1831)

Sumner, George Henry, *Life of Charles Richard Sumner, D.D.* (London: John Murray, 1876)

Whittingham, Ferdinand (editor), *A Memoir of the Services of Lieutenant-*

Select bibliography

General Sir Samuel Ford Whittingham (London: Longmans, Green, and Co., new edition 1868)

Wilkins, W. H., *Mrs. Fitzherbert and George IV,* 2 volumes (London: Longmans, Green, and Co., 1905)

Williamson, George C., and Henry L. D. Engleheart, *George Engleheart, 1750–1829. Miniature Painter to George III* (London: George Bell, 1902)

Wilson, Frances, *The Courtesan's Revenge. Harriette Wilson, the Woman who Blackmailed the King* (London: Faber and Faber, 2004)

Local

Baillie, Alexander F., *The Oriental Club and Hanover Square* (London: Longmans, Green, and Co., 1901)

Beddow, J. C., *A History of Bere Ferrers Parish*, 3rd edition (Privately published by the author, 1995)

Gill, Crispin, *Plymouth. A New History*, volume 2 of 2, *1603 to the Present Day* (Newton Abbot: David and Charles, 1979)

Gray, Todd, and Margery Rowe, *Travels in Georgian Devon. The Illustrated Journals of the Reverend John Swete, 1781–1800*, volume 1 of 4 (Tiverton: Devon Books/Halsgrove)

Jones, Steve, *Admiral Sir Charles Napier and Merchistoun Hall* (Havant: Fuchsia Publications, 2004)

Sheppard, Edgar, *Memorials of St James's Palace,* 2 volumes (London: Longmans, Green, and Co., 1894)

Sheppard, F. H. W. (editor), *Survey of London,* volume 31, part 2, *The Parish of St James Westminster. North of Piccadilly* (London: Athlone Press/London County Council, 1963)

Taylor, John George, *Our Lady of Battersea: The Story of Battersea Church and Parish Told from Original Sources* (Chelsea: George White, 1925)

Thornbury, Walter, *Old and New London. A Narrative of its History, its People and its Places*, 6 volumes (London, Paris and New York: Cassell, Peter, and Galpin, 1879)

Worth, R. N., *History of the Town and Borough of Devonport, sometime*

Plymouth Dock (Plymouth, W. Brendon and Son; Devonport: S. G. Pyke, 1870)

Medical

Blandy, John P., and John S. P. Lumley (editors), *The Royal College of Surgeons of England: 200 Years of History at the Millennium* (London: Royal College of Surgeons/Blackwell Science, 2000)

Clark, Sir George, *A History of the Royal College of Physicians of London*, volume 2 of 4 (Oxford: Clarendon Press for the Royal College of Physicians, 1966)

Howard, Martin, *Wellington's Doctors. The British Army Medical Services in the Napoleonic Wars* (Staplehurst: Spellmount, 2002)

Lawrence, Susan C., *Charitable Knowledge. Hospital pupils and practitioners in eighteenth-century London* (Cambridge: Cambridge University Press, 1996)

Lewis, Judith Schneid, *In the Family Way. Childbearing in the British Aristocracy, 1760–1860* (New Brunswick, New Jersey: Rutgers University Press, 1986)

Lloyd, Christopher, and Jack L. S. Coulter, *Medicine and the Navy 1200–1900*, volume 3 of 4, *1714–1815* (Edinburgh and London: E. and S. Livingstone Ltd, 1961)

Loudon, Irvine, *Medical Care and the General Practitioner, 1750–1850* (Oxford: Clarendon Press, 1986)

Porter, Dorothy, and Roy Porter, *Patient's Progress. Doctors and Doctoring in Eighteenth-century England* (Oxford: Polity Press, 1989)

Knighton, William, *Observations on the Use of Mercury in Putrid Fevers, and the Putrid and Ulcerated Sore Throat* (Devonport, c1800)

Rodger, N. A. M., *The Wooden World. An Anatomy of the Georgian Navy* (London: Collins, 1986)

Rosner, Lisa, *Medical Education in the Age of Improvement: Edinburgh Students and Apprentices, 1760–1826* (Edinburgh University Press, 1991)

Turnbull, William, *The Naval Surgeon; comprising the entire duties of*

Select bibliography

professional men at sea, to which are subjoined, a system of naval surgery, and a compendious pharmacopoeia (London: Richard Phillips, 1806)

Army and navy

Berry, Robert Potter, *A History of the Formation and Development of The Volunteer Infantry, from the Earliest Times, Illustrated by the Local Records of Huddersfield and its Vicinity From 1794 to 1874* (London: Simpkin, Marshall, Hamilton, Kent and Co.; Huddersfield: J. Broadbent and Co., 1903)

Gee, Austin, *The British Volunteer Movement, 1794–1814* (Oxford: Clarendon Press, 2003)

Linch, Kevin B., '"A Citizen and Not a Soldier": The British Volunteer Movement and the War against Napoleon', in Alan Forrest, Karen Hagemann and Jane Rendall (editors), *Soldiers, Citizens and Civilians. Experiences and Perceptions of the Revolutionary and Napoleonic Wars, 1790–1820* (Basingstoke and New York: Palgrave Macmillan, 2009), pages 206–221

Rodger, N. A. M., *The Command of the Ocean. A Naval History of Britain, 1649–1815* (London: Allen Lane/National Maritime Museum, 2004)

Stout, Neil R., *The Royal Navy in America, 1760–1775* (Annapolis, Maryland: Naval Institute Press, 1973)

National and international

Aspinall, A., *Politics and the Press c.1780–1850* (London: Home and Van Thal, 1949)

Grenville, Richard, the Duke of Buckingham and Chandos, *Memoirs of the Court of England during The Regency, 1811–1820. From original family documents*, volume 1 of 2 (London: Hurst and Blackett, 1856)

Price, Roger, *A Concise History of France*, 2nd edition (Cambridge: Cambridge University Press, 2005)

Temperley, Harold, *The Foreign Policy of Canning, 1822–1827. England, the Neo-Holy Alliance, and the New World,* 2nd edition (London: Frank Cass and Co. Ltd, 1966)

Royal

Anon, *The Royal Criterion* (1814)

Crook, Maudaunt J., and M. H. Port, *The History of the King's Works*, volume 6 of 6, *1782–1851* (London: Her Majesty's Stationery Office, 1973)

Hartop, Christopher, Diana Scarisbrick, Charles Truman, David Watkin and Matthew Winterbottom, *Royal Goldsmiths: The Art of Rundell and Bridge, 1797–1843* (Cambridge: John Adamson for Koopman Rare Art, 2005)

Goodwin, Albert, 'War Transport and "Counter-revolution" in France in 1793: the Case of the Winter Company and the Financier Jean-Jacques de Beaune', in M. R. D. Foot (editor), *War and Society. Historical essays in honour and memory of J. R. Western 1928–1971* (London: Paul Elek, 1973)

Hedley, Olwen, *Royal Palaces* (London: Robert Hale, 1972)

Sheppard, Edgar, *Memorials of St. James's Palace,* 2 volumes (London and New York: Longmans, Green, and Co., 1894)

Somerville, Sir Robert, *History of the Duchy of Lancaster,* volume 2 of 2, *1603–1965* (London: The Chancellor and Council of the Duchy of Lancaster, 2000)

Williams, Neville, *Royal Homes of Great Britain, from medieval to modern times* (London: Lutterworth Press, 1971)

Carlton House. The Past Glories of George IV's Palace (London: The Queen's Gallery, Buckingham Palace, 1991) [exhibition catalogue]

Georgian life

Ehrman, Edwina, Hazel Forsyth, Lucy Peltz and Cathy Ross, *London Eats Out: 500 Years of Capital Dining* (London: Museum of London/Philip Wilson Publishers, 1999) [exhibition catalogue]

Hope, Ronald, *A New History of British Shipping* (London: John Murray, 1990)

Sprang, Rebecca L., *The Invention of the Restaurant: Paris and Modern Gastronomic Culture* (Cambridge, Massachusetts, and London: Harvard University Press, 2000)

Select bibliography

Reference

Anderson, Peter John (editor), *Officers and graduates of University and King's College, Aberdeen, 1495–1860* (Aberdeen: New Spalding Club, 1893)

Colvin, Howard (editor), *A Biographical Dictionary of British Architects, 1600–1840*, 3rd edition (Newhaven and London: Yale University Press, 1995)

Houfe, Simon (editor), *The Dictionary of 19th Century British Book Illustrators and Caricaturists* (Woodbridge, Suffolk; The Antique Collectors' Club, 1996)

Pevsner, Nikolaus, and David Lloyd, *The Buildings of England: Hampshire and the Isle of Wight* (Harmandsworth: Penguin Books, 1967)

Pevsner, Nikolaus, and Bridget Cherry, *The Buildings of England: Devon*, 2nd edition (London: Penguin Books, 1989)

Sainty, J. C., and R. O. Bucholz (editors), Office-Holders in Modern Britain, volume 11, Officials of the Royal Household, 1660–1837. Part I: Department of the Lord Chamberlain and associated offices (London: University of London/Institute of Historical Research, 1997)

Sainty, J. C., and R. O. Bucholz (editors), Office-Holders in Modern Britain, volume 12, Officials of the Royal Household, 1660–1837. Part 2: Departments of the Lord Steward and the Master of the Horse (London: University of London/Institute of Historical Research, 1998)

Somerville, Sir Robert, *Office-Holders in the Duchy and County Palatine of Lancaster from 1603* (London and Chichester: Phillimore, 1972)

Wallis, P. J., and R. V. Wallis, *Eighteenth Century Medics (subscriptions, licences, apprenticeships)*, 2nd edition (Newcastle upon Tyne: Project for Historical Bibliography, 1988)

Benezit Dictionary of Artists (Paris: Gründ, 2006)
Boyle's Court Guide
Crosby's Merchant's and Tradesman's Pocket Dictionary
Dictionary of Architecture (Architectural Publication Society, 1848)

Extraordinary Black Book
Holden's Triennial Directory
Imperial Calendar
List of the Officers of the Several Regiments and Corps of Fencible Cavalry and Infantry: of the Officers of the Militia, of the Corps and Troops of Gentlemen and Yeomanry, and of the Corps and Companies of Volunteer Infantry (War Office)
Manual of Rank and Nobility (London: Saunders and Otley, 1828)
Munk's Roll
Royal Kalendar
Underhill's Directory

Maps

Greenwood, J., and C. Greenwood, map of Hampshire (1826)
The A to Z of Regency London (Lympne Castle, Kent: Harry Margary/ Guildhall Library London, 1985)
Stuart, Elizabeth, *Lost Landscapes of Plymouth* (Stroud: Alan Sutton/Map Collector Publications Ltd, 1991)
Blendworth and Catherington enclosure maps (1816)
Blendworth tithe map (1838)
Plymouth and Launceston 1809–1813 (Timeline Maps Ltd, 2006)

Articles

Aspinall, Arthur, 'George IV and Sir William Knighton', *English Historical Review,* volume 55, No 217 (Jan 1940) pages 57–82
Lane, Joan, 'Provincial Medical Apprentices and Masters in Early Modern England', *Eighteenth Century Life* (Pittsburgh*)*, volume 12, part 3 (1988), pages 4–27
Maxted, Ian, *Cider and eighteenth century evidence based healthcare. A Devon pamphlet war* from http://bookhistory.blogspot.com
Morris, W. I. C., 'Sir William Knighton. The Invisible Accoucheur', *Manchester Medical Gazette,* volume 55, part 2 (1976), pages 46–50

Select bibliography

Lloyd, Christopher, 'George IV, Sir William Knighton and Sir David Wilkie', *Apollo*, volume 156, issue 486 (August 2002), pages 53–55

Millar, G. T., 'James Wardrop (1782–1869): from Whitburn to Windsor Castle', *Historical Review,* from www.rcs.ed.ac.uk/Journal/Volume46

Wall, J. R., 'The Guy's Hospital Physical Society (1771–1852)', *Guy's Hospital Reports*, volume 123 (1974), pages 159–170

Unpublished

Christie, Manson and Woods, Messrs., *Catalogue of the service of plate, gold snuff-boxes, watches and miniatures, bronzes, porcelain, clocks, engravings, water-colour drawings and collection of ancient and modern pictures, of Sir William W. Knighton, Bart., deceased, late of Blendworth Lodge, Hants* (1885)

Culpin, R. T., *Two Hundred Years of a Local Family* [Clarke Jervoise] (Cheriton: 1996)

Doran, W., *The only authentic edition of the Memoirs of the life of Philip Rundell....* (Typescript of Doran's 1827 publication)

Fox, George, *An account of the firm of Rundell, Bridge & Co., the Crown Jewellers and goldsmiths on Ludgate Hill* (1840s)

Larks, G. E., *The Plymouth Medical Society in the Nineteenth Century*. A paper read to the Plymouth Medical Society on 23 February 1968

Moore, Violet Marie, *Wolff Family* (1915)

Newspapers, magazines and journals

Christian Reformer
Court Magazine and Monthly Critic
Exeter Flying Post
Hampshire Telegraph
Lancet
London Gazette
Monthly Gazette of Health
Quarterly Review
The Times

Electronic

www.familysearch.org

http://hansard.millbanksystems.com

http://infotrac.galegroup.com

www.internationalbyronsociety.org

www.london-gazette.co.uk

www.oxforddnb.com

www.proni.gov.uk

http://royalsocietypublishing.org

Select bibliography

Archival

British Library	Correspondence with Richard Wellesley, Thomas Byam Martin and Richard Bentley, publisher; Northcote's autobiography; volunteer lists
Caird Library, National Maritime Museum	Transcript of Richard Creyke's journal
Centre for Buckinghamshire Studies	Ward family archive
Devon Record Office	Bere Ferrers parish records, including rates and apprenticeships; land tax; Dorothy Toll's will
Guildhall Library	Insurance policies
Hampshire Record Office	Blendworth diocesan and civil records, Dr K. S. Southam's notes; Clarke Jervoise archives; Knollis correspondence, Blendworth land tax
Havant Museum	Richard Culpin's MS
King's College, London	Guy's Physical Society
Lambeth Archives Department, Minet Library	Jens Wolff
London Metropolitan Archives	Middlesex Deeds Registry
Museum of English Rural Life	Luscombe correspondence
The National Archives	Granville archive; Lord Chamberlain's and Lord Steward's Departments; Wolff bankruptcy; Pierre Lacroix's reports; Plymouth Hospital Muster Books; Foreign Office reports

National Art Library, Victoria and Albert Museum	Prout correspondence, Rundell biographies
Plymouth Local Studies	Plymouth Medical Society
Plymouth and West Devon Record Office	Bere Ferrers civil records; Plymouth Medical Society; Plymouth rent books; Treby archive; estate survey of James Young's lands in Bere Ferrers; Whitchurch parish records; Luxes Park
Portsmouth City Records Office	Blendworth parish records
Royal Academy	Lawrence correspondence
Royal Archives	Knighton's diary 1–21 February 1830
Royal College of Physicians	1807 meeting; College Annals
Royal College of Surgeons	Company of Surgeons examination books; Corporation of Surgeons lists; Pemberton correspondence
Surrey History Centre	Sherwood Lodge catalogue; Battersea parish rates and land tax
Wandsworth Local History Service, Battersea Library	Battersea rates, Jens Wolff; Sherwood Lodge
Wellcome Library	Knighton's article on the use of mercury
West Country Studies Centre	Parish files; *Exeter Flying Post*
West Sussex Record Office	Correspondence of Anne Grey; Will of William Thomas Williams
Westminster City Archives	Parish rates for St James's and Hanover Square; Parish registers for Hanover Square; Reverend Sanderson Robins

INDEX

It is recommended that index users are familiar with the "Who's Who" section on
pages xi–xiii of the introduction to avoid confusion.

accoucheur, job description 35–6
Adolphus, Duke of Cambridge xiv, 72
Aimsworth, Charles 20
Arbuthnot, Charles 73, 76, 87
Arbuthnot, Harriett 73, 125
Argyll Street 23
Ashdon 6, 17–18

Bagot, Charles 90–1
baronetcy 39–40
Bayleys 6, 17–18
de Beaune affair 94–7
Bere Ferrers 1, 17–18
Blendworth 57–62, 65–7, 137, 145–7, 152
Bloomfield, Benjamin 46–7, 51–3
Boyles, Reverend Charles Gower 59, 137
Bredall, William 4, 7–9, 20, 37
Brodie, Benjamin 33, 36, 111–12, 123
Brougham, Henry 49, 73, 96, 123
Byam Martin, Thomas 36

Cambridge, Duke of (Adolphus) xiv, 72
Canning, George 30–1, 33, 74, 77, 81–2, 85–9
Caroline of Brunswick, Princess 46, 47–9
Chambers, William 113
Charlotte, Princess 47
Charlotte, Queen 47

Clarence, Duke of (William) xiv, 93–5, 145
Clarke, Samuel. *See* Jervoise, Reverend Sir Samuel Clarke
Continental journeys 70–2, 77–80, 82–5, 89–91, 95–100, 101–2
Conyngham, Albert 82–3
Conyngham, Elizabeth 70, 72, 75, 77–8, 90, 108
Conyngham, Henry 77–9
Coulthred, Reverend John 59
Creyke, Richard 15–16
Cullen, Peter 13–14
Cumberland, Duke of (Ernest) xiv, 72, 98–9

Danvers, Frederick 117
de Beaune affair 94–7
Douglas, Sally 28–9, 128–9
Duchy of Cornwall 44, 47, 70, 115–17, 144
Duchy of Lancaster 70, 83, 115–17, 144
Duncombe, Thomas 92, 136

Edinburgh University 25–6
Ernest, Duke of Cumberland xiv, 72, 98–9

father Knighton (1738–1830) xi, 1, 5, 110
Fitzherbert, Maria 46, 48, 130–1
foreign trips 67
    to the Continent 70–2, 77–80,

169

82–5, 89–91, 95–100, 101–2
  to the Peninsula 31–3
  after retirement 139
  to Scotland 54
Frederick, Duke of York xiv, 72, 76, 85–6, 88, 93–95
Frogstreet 2, 5–6

Geach, Francis 9, 17–18, 19–20
George III 47
George IV 38–9, 43–55, 81–100, 101–9, 132–136
  siblings xiii–xiv, 72
George Street 127, 142
Gooch, Robert 26, 48, 82, 105, 113
grandfather Knighton xi, 2–4, 5–6, 17
Grenofen 2–4
Grey, Anne 119–20
Guy's Hospital 10–13
Guy's Physical Society 12–13

Hallifax, Robert 39
Hammick, Stephen 9, 15, 112–13
Hanover 49–51, 67, 71–2
Hanover Square 29–30, 108–9, 127
Hawker, Captain James 20–1
Hawker, Dorothea. See Knighton, Dorothea (wife)
Hill, Dorothy. See mother Knighton
hospitals
  Guy's 10–13
  Royal Naval 15–17, 126
  St Thomas's 10–13
Huxham, John 11, 20

Jenkinson, Robert Banks xiii, 75, 79, 86–7
Jervoise, Reverend Sir Samuel Clarke 57–9, 61, 145–6
journeys abroad. See foreign trips

King's College, Aberdeen 26, 127
Knighton, Dora xii, 31, 65, 102, 105
Knighton, Dorothea (wife) 20–3, 27, 55–6, 62, 124–5, 128
  drawings by 151, 152
Knighton, Dorothy. See mother Knighton (Dorothy)
Knighton, Frances 7, 8–9
Knighton, John Moore 2, 3, 7, 17
Knighton, Mary Frances 41, 62
Knighton, William (1801–1802) xi, 23
Knighton, William (c1716–1784). See grandfather Knighton
Knighton, William (c1738–1780). See father Knighton
Knighton, William (c1777–1836) xi
  baronetcy 39–40
  homes of 129–31
    Argyll Street 23
    Blendworth 48, 56–62, 65–7, 137, 145–7
    George Street 127, 142
    Hanover Square 29–30, 108–9, 127
    Sherwood Lodge 40–1, 48, 151
  Stratford Place 139
  illness and death 80, 86–7, 101, 103, 146, 148–9
  marriage 20–1
  medical career 35–9, 55
Knighton, William Wellesley xi, 40, 41, 62, 83–4, 141–2, 147–8

Lawrence, Thomas 75–6, 103, 117

Index

Le Marchant, Sir Denis 122
Luke, Stephen 20
Luxes Park 6, 17–18

McMahon, John 42, 43–5, 52, 96
  McMahon papers 132–3
Marrable, Thomas 43, 45, 111
Memoirs, The xiv–xv, 5, 124–5
mercury, use in medicine 37
Metzler, Jane 62, 64, 121
Milan Commission 48–9
Milman, Sir Francis 23
mother Knighton (Dorothy) xii, 3–4, 6, 36, 49, 63–4

Naval Surgeon, The 16
Northcote, James 27, 68, 103, 145

Peninsula visits 31–3
Plymouth Medical Society 19–20
Pope, Alexander 19
Princess Caroline of Brunswick 46, 47–9
Princess Charlotte 47
Privy Council 52, 75

Quarterly Review, The 83
Queen Charlotte 47

Regency Memoirs 34
Robinson, Frederick John xiii, 89, 91
Roman Catholic emancipation 85–6, 87, 99
Royal College of Physicians 23–4
Royal Criterion, The 93–5
Royal Naval Hospital 15–17, 126

St Andrews University 17, 20, 127

St Thomas's Hospital 10–13
Sarson, George 61
Scott, John xiii, 74–5
Scott, Walter 39, 54, 68, 109, 145
Seymour, Captain Michael (Michael) xiii, 65, 143, 147
Seymour, Dora xii, 31, 65, 102, 105
Seymour, James 122
Seymour, Little Dora xii, 105–6
Seymour, Rear-Admiral Sir Michael (Seymour) xiii, 60–1, 137, 143, 146
Sherwood Lodge 40–1, 151
Southey, Henry 26, 113
Spanish trips 31–3
Stratford Place 139
Sumner, Charles 65, 72–3, 79, 114, 121, 122–3
Sydenham, Benjamin 31–2

Toll, Dorothy. *See* mother Knighton
Toll, James 6, 64
Tolle, John 63–4, 117, 122
Treby family 118–19
Tupper, Martin 113
Turnbull, William 16
Turner, Richard 4

Ultras 73–4
University of Edinburgh 25–6
University of St Andrews 17, 20, 127
Ward, John William 89–91
Wardrop, James 54, 106–7, 108
Weekes, Hampton 10–12
Wellesley, Arthur xiii, 28
  politics 73, 78–9, 91, 140
  tensions with Knighton 87–8, 102, 104

Wellesley, Henry 32, 82
Wellesley, Hyacinthe 29, 129
Wellesley, Richard xiii, 28–9, 30–3, 38–9, 41–2, 98, 129
Whittingham, Samuel Ford 114, 122
Wilkie, David 118, 142
William, Duke of Clarence xiv, 72, 93–5, 145
Wilson, Harriette 84, 85, 90–1, 102, 131–2, 135–6
Wolff, Jens 41

York, Duke of (Frederick) xiv, 72, 76, 85–6, 88, 93–5